Preface

No, this is NOT a cookbook!

In March 2020, as the reality of COVID-19 hit home, I started baking challah, the delicious, braided egg bread that is typically eaten on the Sabbath and other important Jewish holidays. More importantly, I started **WRITING** about baking challah. Getting inspiration from England's World War II rallying cry, I searched the internet and found Keep Calm Maker on Zazzle, an American on-line marketplace, could create an apron with a *Keep Calm and Bake Challah* logo embroidered on the top half. The yellow cotton pinafore arrived in June and my wearing it while baking the loaves became as necessary to the process as kneading the flour, sugar, salt, oil, and yeast. I knew that the mantra would be the title of my book.

Over the next two and half years, I wrote about baking challah. I also wrote about adjusting to the "new normal." Wearing masks. Zooming with family and friends. Missing in-person birthdays, bar and bat mitzvahs, graduations, weddings, and funerals. Following the news as the country was split apart. And finally emerging slowly back into life more closely resembling the pre-COVID years.

In April 2023, my editor Mia Crews and I were putting the final touches on *Keep Calm and Bake Challah* before publication. We were going back and forth with necessary changes to the fifty-three stories as well as the cover, which featured a picture of me wearing my apron and holding a huge, braided loaf. Finally, Mia uploaded the first draft copy of the book. That Friday afternoon, I greeted the deliveryman as he handed me the brown envelope that held my new "baby."

"Thank you so much!" I told him. "It's my book!"

"That's nice," he said, as he turned around and started heading for his truck.

"No, it's not any book," I said. "It's **my** book! I wrote it. Do you want to see it?"

Before he could answer, I tore open the envelope and showed him the proof copy.

"That's nice," he said. "You wrote a cookbook."

"No, it's **NOT** a cookbook," I said. "It's a collection of stories about my life during the pandemic."

As he left, however, I took a closer look at the cover. It DID look like a cookbook. That opinion was confirmed by several other people to whom I showed the proof.

Over that weekend, I agonized over my dilemma. Did I need a new cover? A new title? Or did I need to throw out hundreds of hours of writing and editing, keep the cover and title, and just write a cookbook? I seriously considered a title change—*Thankful? Finding a Silver Lining?*—until a conversation with five of my cousins on our weekly Tuesday Zoom call.

"Don't change the title," they said. "Just put a banner proclaiming, 'No! This is NOT a cookbook!'"

I gladly followed their advice. I had been working on this book since March 2020, and I knew that the chosen title best reflected all those months of dealing with the pandemic. More importantly, I **loved** the title. No matter how many people passed up on my book because it looks like a cookbook, at least the title and cover would be what I dreamt it would be from the beginning of this journey.

So I proudly present *Keep Calm and Bake Challah: How I Survived the Pandemic, Politics, Pratfalls, and Other of Life's Problems.* For all of you who thought this was a cookbook, I hope you enjoy it anyway. And to make everyone happy, my challah recipe is included at the end of this book. Happy baking!

Happy reading!

Marilyn Cohen Shapiro

Keep Calm
and
Bake Challah

How I Survived the Pandemic, Politics, Pratfalls, and Other of Life's Problems

Marilyn Cohen Shapiro

Keep Calm and Bake Challah:©

How I Survived the Pandemic, Politics, Pratfalls, and Other of Life's Problems

Editor: Mia Crews
Staff artist: Maria Eames
Cover photo of author by Larry Shapiro.

Family photos from the author's private collection.

Many of these stories first appeared in *The Jewish World* (http://jewishworldnews.org) and the *Heritage Florida Jewish News* under the name Marilyn Shapiro. The author has tried to recreate events, locales, and conversations from her memories of them to the best of her ability. Some of the names have been changed; real names are used with permission.

The author may be contacted via email at *shapcomp18@gmail.com.*

Dedication

This book is dedicated to my children,
Adam, Julie, Sam, and Sarah

and to my grandchildren,
Sylvie Rose, Sidney Ellis, and Frances June

The best things in life are the people we love,
the places we've been,
and the memories we've made along the way.
Unknown

Acknowledgements

Thanks to our siblings and their spouses and partners, who, thanks to a pandemic, got closer through Zoom calls: Laura Appel and Will Kocsovsky; Anita and Burt Beck; Jay and Leslie Cohen, Marilyn Pearl Shapiro, and Howard Stark; Bobbie and Emil Chiauzzi, and Carole and Bill Leakakos.

Thanks to our Tuesday Night Cousin's Zoom for shedding light on and life into our complex and wonderful family tree. A special shout-out to Ellen Hurwitch, who organized the calls, and to my brother Jay, who organized the family tree.

Thanks to the members of my two book clubs, Book Babes and Clifton Park Hadassah Book Club, who provided hours of quality reading and interesting Zoom discussions.

Thanks to my mah-jongg group. Those Friday mornings sitting in our lawn chairs under the trees for a huge chunk of the pandemic kept our sisterhood thriving. Glad we are back to playing! Mary Buck, Marcia Figenholtz, Hedy Flechner, Wendy Nowak, Sharon Ranonis, Mayra Skeet, and Jenny Suarez.

Thanks to the current and past members of SOL Writers. It was your encouragement that pushed me to publish four books since 2016.

Thanks to all my friends and family who offered suggestions on how to improve my writing.

Thanks to Laurie and Jim Clevenson of the Capital Region of New York's *The Jewish World* for publishing many of the stories in this book.

Thanks to Mia Crews, my editor, for bringing this project to life.

Thanks to my children, Adam, Julie, Sam, and Sarah, whose FaceTime calls got us through the lonely months of the pandemic.

Thanks to my grandchildren, Sylvie, Sidney, and Frances, who light up our lives on FaceTime and in our arms.

And a special thanks to Larry Shapiro, my husband, my soulmate, my best friend, my muse, and the best person in the world with whom to go through a pandemic.

Contents

Definitions of Jewish Words

Aliyah: Immigration to Israel by Jewish person

Ashkenazi: Jewish person of Eastern European descent; usually speaker of Yiddish

Bar/Bat Mitzvah: Jewish religious ritual and family celebration commemorating the religious adulthood of a boy on his 13th birthday. Known as bat mitzvah for girl

Bereishit: First book of the Torah; Genesis

Bialy: Breakfast roll with depressed center covered with onion flakes

Bisl: Little, small,few

Bubbe: Grandmother

Chag Sameach: Happy Holiday!

Challah: Braided egg bread eaten on Shabbat and other Jewish holidays.

Charotzes: Mixture of nuts, apples, and wine served on Passover

Chometz: Leaven bread and food banned on Passover

Chuppah: Ceremonial canopy used at Jewish weddings

Chutzpah: Nerve

Der Forvert: *The Jewish Forward;* Yiddish newspaper founded in 1897.

Farklempt: Overcome with emotion

Hadassah: International women's Zionist organization that supports numerous Jewish causes as well as its eponymous Jerusalem hospital

Haftorah: A series of selections from the book of Prophets read in synagogue along with Torah portion

Haggadah: Book of readings for Passover seder

Haman: Bad guy in Purim story

Hamantaschen: Three cornered jam-filled cookies traditionally eaten on Purim.

Hanukkah: Jewish festival commemorating the recovery of Jerusalem, subsequent rededication of the Second Temple; Maccabean victory against Seleucid Empire in 2nd century BCE.

Hanukkiah: Nine-branched candleholder used on Hanukkah.

Kabbalah: Jewish mysticism

Kaddish: Prayer said at Jewish services by mourners of close relative

Keppie: Yiddish for Head

Kiddish: (Holiness) Prayer over wine (or grape juice) that sanctifies Shabbat and holidays.

Kike: Contemptuous name for Jewish person

Kishki: Beef or fowl casing stuffed and cooked

Kol Nidre: Opening service of Yom Kippur

Kosher: Selling or serving of food that follows Jewish dietary laws

Kugel: Pudding, most notably luchen (noodle) and potato.

Kvetch: Complain

Kvell: Be proud; rejoice

L'Chaim: To Life!

Latke: Pancake

L'Shana Tova: "Have a good year!"

Matzah: Unleavened bread eaten on Passover

Matzah brie: Fried matzah

Mazel Tov: Good Luck! Also, Congratulations!

Megillah: Book read on Purim

Mensch: A good person

Meshugganah: Crazy

Midrash: Tale, story

Mispachah: Jewish family or social unit including close/distant relatives

Mishagas: Confusion

Mi Shebeirach: Prayer of Healing

Neshome: Soul

Pesach: Passover, Jewish holiday that celebrates the Biblical story of the Israelites' escape from slavery in Egypt

Punim: Face

Purim: Jewish holiday which commemorates the saving of the Jewish people from Haman, an official of the empire in 5 BCE, Persian empire who was planning to have all Jewish subjects killed.

Putz: Worthless person

Refuah sh'leimah; Complete healing/recovery

Rosh Hashanah: The Jewish New Year. Usually falls in September or October.

Shabbat: Sabbath. Judaism's day of rest and seventh day of the week. Observed from sundown Friday to sundown Saturday.

Seder: A Jewish ritual feast that marks the beginning of the Jewish holiday of Passover

Shavuot: Day of celebrating giving of the Torah

Shayna kleyna meydl: Pretty little girl

Sh'ma: Prayer that serves as a centerpiece of the morning and evening Jewish prayer services

Shemndrick: Foolish person

Schlepp: Carry, drag, or haul with difficulty

Shtetl: A small Jewish town or village formerly found in Eastern Europe

Simchas Torah: Day of celebrating the Torah

Shiker: Drunk

Shiksa: Non-Jewish girl or woman

Schlemiel: Stupid, awkward person

Schlimazel: Unlucky person

Shmatta: Worn, old piece of clothing

Shofar: Ram's horn traditionally blown on High Holy Days

Shpiel: Skit

Tallit: Shawl with fringed corners worn over the head or shoulders by Jews at services

Talmud: Authoritative written body of Jewish tradition comprising the Mishnah and Gemara

Tchotkes: Trinkets

Tikkun Olam: Jewish concept; suggests humanity's shared responsibility to heal, repair, and transform the world

Torah: Judaism's most important text which contains Five Books of Moses. Read in synagogues on a *Sefer Torah* (Torah scrolls)

Tractates: Short tract, treatise of Talmud

Tsouris: Trouble, distress, problems

Tu B'Shevat: Festival of Trees

Tuches: Rear end; *tushie*

Tzaddik: Righteous person. Plural: *Tzaddikim*

Yibbum: Levirate marriage in which the brother of a deceased man is obliged to marry his brother's widow.

Yid: Jew

Yiddish: Language spoken by Ashkenazi Jews. Mixture of German and Hebrew

Yeshiva: Jewish day school providing secular and religious instruction

Yom Kippur: Day of Atonement. Annual Jewish observance of fasting, prayer, and repentance. Holiest day on the Jewish calendar.

Zayde: Grandfather

Note: Common Hebrew/Yiddish words are italicized the first time they are used and are in regular font in subsequent uses.

Chapter One

Keep Calm And Bake Challah

Every Friday afternoon since the coronavirus disease turned our world upside down, I have been baking fresh *challah*. I revel in the process, the measuring, the gradual rising, and especially the eating of the soft braided bread traditionally served on the Jewish Sabbath. But it has become so much more. As Roche Pinson wrote in her book, *Rising: The Book of Challah*, "We make challah from a place of commitment to nourish ourselves and our families in a way that goes beyond mere physical feeding and watering."

Even though I can't remember the last time I ever baked a challah before March 2020, two pre-pandemic encounters with fresh-out-of-the-oven loaves motivated me. In August 2019, I met my future daughter-in-law's parents, Carol and Dick Nathan, in their home at their weekly *Shabbat* (Sabbath) dinner. Along with the candle lighting and the *kiddish*, we all joined in the prayer over Carol's freshly baked challah, a tradition she has maintained for decades. The taste of her delicious bread stayed with me throughout the coming months.

On one of the last services at our synagogue in Florida before services were suspended, we enjoyed a challah baked by Liz Ross, a fellow congregant. The daughter of a Jewish mother and an Inuit chief, Liz had discovered her spiritual roots as an adult. As the only Jew in Unalakleet, Alaska, her only choice was to make her own challah to accompany her holiday meals. Years of experience yielded wonderful, sweet bread.

On that first quarantined Friday, I decided a homemade challah would be a perfect comfort food. I pulled out my friend Flo Miller's challah recipe that I had stored in a recipe file for years and gathered all the necessary ingredients: yeast, flour, sugar, butter. I mixed and kneaded the sticky dough with my KitchenAid's dough hook and covered it with a cloth tea towel. After it had risen, I shaped the dough into three challahs, brushed on the egg wash, and let it rise again. Once out of the oven, Larry and I dropped off one of the loaves on the doorstep of a friend who was spending Shabbat alone as his wife was in isolation in the memory unit of a nearby nursing home.

As the two loaves waited under my mother's challah cross stitch covering, I lit the Shabbat candles that we had placed in my Grandma Annie's brass candlesticks. Larry recited the Kiddish over the Manischewitz wine, and then we both recited the *HaMotzi* blessing over the warm braided bread. We sat down to our first pandemic Shabbat dinner.

The following week, Larry and I headed to Publix at 7 a.m. as part of a "seniors only" shopping trip. I immediately headed to the baking aisle to stock up on my bread making supplies. I obviously was not the only one needing to knead. Yeast, like toilet paper and hand sanitizers, had completely disappeared from the shelves, with flour, sugar, and eggs in short supply. We grabbed what we could and headed home.

Fortunately, the flour, sugar, and egg situation improved. Initial attempts to purchase yeast online, however, were miserably unsuccessful. Amazon offered a three-pack of Fleischmann's for $25, price gouging at its worst. I sent out an all-points bulletin on Facebook, and three friends dropped off some packets they had in their cupboards. They each got a challah in return. Soon after, Amazon offered a one-pound bag of yeast. Despite the fact it was twice the normal price, I snapped it up.

Thus began my Friday ritual of making the bread and giving one or two of my loaves to others. As a thank-you for two homemade masks. As a *mazel tov* on finishing chemotherapy. As a wish for safe travels to a summer home. If the bread came out of the oven too late for delivery before sundown, we dropped it off the next day with a suggestion to warm it up, toast it, or make it into French toast.

Each week, I tweaked the process. Too much flour made the bread tough. An extra egg yolk made for a richer taste. Covering the bowl with a tea towel and then loosely wrapping it in a clean white kitchen trash bag helped in the rising. Slamming the ball of dough on the counter a few times removed extra gases—and relieved tension! Raisins were a wonderful addition. Creating a challah with six braids or more would take more practice.

One night, when an afternoon nap killed chances for my normal bedtime, I went on YouTube and found a series of challah baking videos made by Jamie Geller, who the Miami Herald calls the "*Kosher* Rachel Ray." An Orthodox Jew who made *aliyah* to Israel in 2012 with her husband and six children, Jamie's demonstration added a spiritual component that touched me. Although she is a professed "shortcut queen," Jamie said she eschews a dough hook in favor of kneading the bread by hand to infuse her love into the loaves. She uses that time to pray for her children, her family, for people in need of *r'fuah sh'leimah,* complete healing.

The next Friday, I used an electric mixer to start the process but then turned the dough onto my floured countertop. Like Jaime, I prayed for my children and grandchildren, who are physically so far away but always in my heart. I prayed for the well-being of my friends and family. I prayed for my friend Kathy who was recovering from COVID-19. I prayed for Minnie, a beautiful baby born at 29 weeks who spent her first weeks of life in a NICU unit. I prayed for Jesse, who just lost his wife to cancer. I prayed for the sick, the grieving, the lonely, the unemployed, the hungry. I prayed for all those impacted by COVID-19. Was it my imagination, or did the challah taste especially sweet, especially delicious that Friday night?

As the Pandemic Panic has moved into the Pandemic New Normal, the need for prayers continues. Our country is marked with severe political divides, strife, and protests—both peaceful and violent. Our world has been rocked with climate catastrophes and wars. So, each Friday, I knead my challah dough, incorporating prayers of hope and healing. And as the beautiful, sweet, braided loaves fill my kitchen with their tantalizing aroma, I will be grateful that my family and I have survived all that the world has thrown on us since COVID-19.

Blessed are You, Adonai our God, Sovereign of all,
who brings forth bread from the earth.
Amen

September 29, 2022

Chapter Two

Yiddish

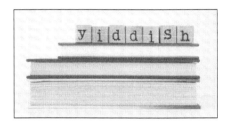

As a blogger and contributor to Jewish newspapers and websites, my articles often include Hebrew and/or Yiddish words. Understanding that people may not be familiar with these languages, I have made a concerted effort to make sure that I defined those words in the context of the sentence.

I thought I had done a good job until a friend told me that she had difficulty with some of the "Jewish" words in my first book, *There Goes My Heart*. She was especially puzzled by one of my food references. "You talked about your husband Larry enjoying a Jewish drink at an Upstate New York deli, something called a Fribble. *"* I smiled and explained a Fribble was extra thick milk shake, one of the specialties served at Friendly's, a Massachusetts-based restaurant chain famous for its ice cream. Nothing *Yiddish* about it, unless you consider it as dairy, not meat!

What is Yiddish? It is the historical language of the *Ashkenazi* Jews. With roots dating back to the seventh century, it is a mixture of high German as well as Hebrew, Aramaic, Slavic, and even Romance languages. I recently read an article in the *Forward* that the Oxford English Dictionary has released its new words and phrases for this quarter, and no less than 71 are Jewish related. Some will make you cheer: *bialy*, *hanukkiah*, and my favorite, Jewish penicillin.

Some, however, will make you jeer. One of the controversial choices is a variation of *Yid—Yiddo*—which is defined as "fans of the British Tottenham Hotspurs soccer team." Responding to debate, the dictionary's compilers said they judge proposed additions by their significance, not whether they offend. In an interview on NPR, television writer Ivor Baddiel called the entry a "step backwards," especially in light of the increased anti-Semitism around the world.

My own introduction to Yiddish came early in my life. My maternal grandparents, who immigrated from Russia circa 1900, spoke Yiddish in their home their entire lives. Their English was weak and heavily accented, and their chief source of news was the Yiddish language paper, *Der Forvert*. My mother spoke fluent Yiddish when she was with her parents, especially when it provided a way for them to gossip about family and friends without worrying that we would understand. Even though his parents also spoke Yiddish, my father never learned the language. That didn't stop him from starting a Yiddish club in their condo in the 1980s. He appointed himself president and assigned my mother to every other office.

As a result, my Yiddish is limited to a *bisl* (few) words that were frequently interspersed in our conversations. My grandmother called me her *shayna kleyna meydl* (pretty little girl). Even after my grandparents passed away, my parents continued to use expressions from the Old Country. A foolish person was a *schmendrick*. When one wasn't *kvetching* (complaining), they were *kvelling* (rejoicing) over their children. And we had to be careful about falling on our *tuches* (rear end) as we could hurt our *keppie* (head).

Larry and his siblings had a similar experience as their maternal grandparents were also Russian immigrants. "Bubbe Rose and Zayde Moshie always spoke Yiddish—especially when they didn't want me to know something," recalled Larry's older sister Anita. "When their friends came over to play cards or Bubbe took me to play bingo, there was always Yiddish interspersed with the English." There was always a Jewish newspaper in the home. Although Moshie passed away when Larry was young, he remembers Bubbe Rose and his parents speaking Yiddish to each other until her passing soon after we were married.

Despite my weak background, I enjoy using Yiddish to spice up my language, especially since many words in Yiddish often surpasses English in its witticism. One of my favorites is the word *chutzpah*. Yes, it may mean "nerve," but nothing catches all the layers than the old story about the child who killed his parents and then pleaded for mercy in court because he was an orphan. Another is the difference between a *schlemiel* and *schlimazel*. The former is the one who drops his soup; the latter is the one on which it lands. Perfect!

Our vocabulary and understanding improved after Leo Rosten published his 1968 book, *The Joys of Yiddish*. I knew few Jewish homes that didn't have a copy of the instant classic on a bookshelf. Larry kept a copy of it in his office desk to assist well-meaning co-workers who would use Yiddish terms incorrectly in their speech or writing.

I also love the beauty of Hebrew words, especially those associated with kindness and compassion. I have used the Hebrew expression for the principle of making the world a better place than when we received it in public speeches, numerous articles, and even the title of my second book, *Tikkun Olam: Stories of Repairing an Unkind World*. Meanwhile, I learned my lesson and made sure to include a glossary of Yiddish and Hebrew words at the beginning of my books.

At times, it is not the written word that trips people up. It is the misinterpretation. Recently, a group of us were talking about how we met our spouses. I shared how Larry and I met at a *Purim* party in Albany, New York. My contribution was met with dead silence, followed by the comment, "I can't believe you told us this!"

"What do you mean?" I asked.

"You met at a **porn** party?" they asked incredulously.

"Oh, no," I responded. "It was a PURIM party!"

After that, I always make sure that I say the name of the Jewish holiday v-e-r-y slowly and clearly!

Larry had no problem deciding that our grandchildren would call him *Zayde*. His father was Zayde to our children, and Larry wanted to continue the tradition. *Bubbe,* however, reminded me of little old ladies in *shmattas* with orthopedic shoes and rolled down hose. With the help of my granddaughter, I became Gammy. But I tell her to watch her *keppie,* and I will *kvetch* when she asks me to *schlepp* too many things home when I pick her up from pre-school. And she will always be, like I was to my own grandmother, my s*hayna kleyna meydl.*

March 19, 2020

Chapter Three

Our First Pandemic Passover

Biblical Irony: Passover seder
may be delayed by the plague.
Facebook meme

Passover, one of Judaism's most important holidays, officially begins with the first *seder* on April 8. *Pesach* in the Time of Coronavirus, however, will be different.

During these difficult times, I think of my parents, Fran and Bill Cohen. As did many of the Greatest Generation, they went through several challenging times. In 1919, the Spanish flu was raging throughout the world. My mother, born in 1917, fell deathly ill. The family doctor saved her life by making a deep incision into her right lung to drain the fluid.

To help in her recovery, my grandmother Ethel left New York City with her daughter for Alburgh, Vermont. They stayed for several weeks with Ethel's brother Paul and his wife Bertie at their home on Lake Champlain. One of their visitors was Ethel's stepmother's sister and her grandson Wilfred Cohen. Fran and Bill didn't meet again until their blind date in 1939. They were married in August 1940. When anyone asked her as to how she got the huge scar on her back, she loved telling people how she survived the flu and met her future husband—all before her second birthday.

Several other cataclysmic events shook their world: The Great Depression, World War II, news of the Holocaust, the atomic bomb, and the Cold War. I am sure at times they were afraid—for themselves and later for their children and grandchildren.

As I write this, we are in the second week of our own national crisis. Larry and I worry about our friends and family—especially our own children. Thankfully, my daughter-in-law delivered our grandson days before the mass shutdowns in San Francisco were enforced. Adam, Sarah, and the baby are now sheltered in place in San Francisco. My heart broke when we had to cancel our trip to meet him. It broke even more when I

17

realized that Sarah's parents, who only live a mile from them, have only seen him through a window when they have dropped off supplies, including a fresh baked challah for his first Shabbat.

Summit County had the first case of the virus in Colorado. A young man who had skied in Italy before his next planned trip to the Rockies recovered in a hospital only a mile from my daughter Julie and her family's home. They returned from a week's vacation with us to closed resorts, schools, and businesses. They too are in mandatory shelter in place mode. They are telecommuting between keeping our granddaughter busy with both educational and fun activities, including learning about the height of a giraffe, the life of a butterfly, and the hands-on steps of baking a challah.

As residents of Florida, Larry and I are not yet under the same mandatory restrictions as California, Colorado, and other areas of the country. But restaurants, non-essential businesses, even Disney World and Universal are now closed down. In our fifty-five plus community, all activities and events have been cancelled or postponed. Most of the people here are respectful of the six-foot-distance rule, which we practice on our frequent bike rides, walks, and conversations with friends from one end of a driveway to the other. We give each other virtual hugs and then head home.

For the rest of the day, we do what we can to keep busy. Larry and I often sit on our lanai, reading books, doing puzzles, and watching birds dive into the pond behind our house. Larry spends a great deal of time Googling great moments in sports and watching reruns of his favorite shows. I spend an inordinate amount of time on Facebook and watching Great Performances on PBS. We call and text with friends. We watch television. On the first Friday of the "new normal," I made a Shabbat dinner, complete with wine and a delicious freshly baked challah—my first since moving down here from New York.

The best part of every day is FaceTiming with our family, an almost daily treat that began on March 14, just before the world changed. Larry and I were planning to go to a play that was being put on by our local theater guild—what was to be our last outing before our own lockdown. Julie, who was worried about our contracting the virus, begged us to stay home. She must have shared her fears with her brother. Shortly before Larry and I were to leave, Adam FaceTimed with us and offered us a sweet deal: If we didn't go out, he would keep the camera on the baby. For the next hour, we watched our six-day-old grandchild poop and pee and eat and sleep and poop some more. With all due respect to my friends in *Deathtrap*, it was one of the best performances we had seen by a leading actor in our lifetime.

Despite the impact the pandemic has had on our lives, I feel undeniably grateful. Grateful for good health with no underlying conditions. Grateful for the current health of extended family and friends. Grateful for modern technology that allows us to connect with our family and friends, to stream shows and movies, to download library books onto our electronic readers. Grateful that we are retired and not dealing with working at home or—worse yet—possible unemployment.

We also feel grateful to have a fully stocked refrigerator and pantry, as not all people have that luxury. Those individuals in our surrounding neighborhoods who are losing income due to the shutdowns could especially use some help. The refund we received from the cancelled Shalom Club *seder* went to the local food bank. As our synagogue had already deposited the check, the board called everyone who was attending to ask if their money could go to the same place. In a recent column in the *Orlando Sentinel*, Scott Maxwell offers many other ways to give to veterans, hungry school children, and the homeless. My favorite of his suggestions: "Did you hoard? Pay it forward." And we all can follow the Center for Disease Control's guidelines and stay home!

So why is this Passover different from every other Passover? We certainly will not be emptying our house of *chometz*, as we have stocked up on many dry goods that certainly don't follow strict *kosher* guidelines. Community seders have already been cancelled. Relatives and friends who usually have a houseful for the holiday will have only two or three at the table, possibly enhanced virtually thanks to FaceTime or Zoom.

No matter, I will make a seder for the two of us. In the days that follow—if we can somehow get more than the two dozen eggs per family limit at the local supermarket—we will feast on sponge cakes, *matzah brie*, and Passover popovers. Most importantly, we will FaceTime with our family and give each other virtual hugs. And Larry and I will pray that the coronavirus will pass over all our homes and leave us, like our ancestors, safe, healthy, and free from fear.

April 3, 2020

Chapter Four

Early Days

A s we tread carefully through the fourth month of the coronavirus pandemic, the emotional and physical devastation this plague has caused is felt acutely by so many. As our days of sheltering at home continue, it has become much more real, much more personal, much more frightening.

Larry and I are feeling the impact, as I suspect many of you are. Our community already has had two confirmed deaths from the virus. Kathy Glascott, a friend from my writing group who had been sick with bronchitis, posted the following message on March 30 on her Facebook page: "I have pneumonia and am in the Poinciana Medical Center where I am getting fantastic care. Take care. Be well." Two days later, her brother Brian Joyce posted that she had been diagnosed with COVID-19 and was on a ventilator. His daily updates report more grim news that she is still fighting for her life.

Friends and family are all sharing stories of people they know who have been diagnosed with the coronavirus and those who have lost the battle. A longtime congregant of our synagogue in Upstate New York succumbed to the virus this week. My son's brother-in-law's grandfather in California died after contracting the virus from his daughter. Each day the numbers continue to climb.

Although most of my friends are retired, many have children on the front line as medical staff or first responders. They post and text pictures of their son or daughter in full protective gear or—worse yet—reused masks and garbage bags for scrubs. Originally, it was believed that the virus mostly attacked the elderly and those with underlying conditions. That reassurance no longer works, and my friends are worried that their children or grandchildren will contract it.

Any medical procedure becomes a cause for serious concern and even panic. A friend scheduled for cancer surgery was terrified that he would develop the virus and would be told he must cancel. When the surgery did go through as scheduled, his wife had to drop him off at the hospital and pick him up two days later. She couldn't physically be there for him.

Another friend, also diagnosed with cancer, was told by her Florida doctor that the surgery would be postponed until the pandemic had subsided. Fortunately, she was able to find a doctor in her hometown of Pittsburgh who could operate within the week. She and her husband made a hasty trip up to Pennsylvania for the procedure. I am happy to report that her surgery was a success.

Soon after, Larry was involved in an accident when the bicycle he was riding skidded out on some wet pavement. Our primary physician insisted Larry go to the emergency room for a tetanus shot and for potential stitches for the gash on his elbow. I freaked out, fearing he would contract the virus in the waiting room. "Please don't go," I begged. "Stay home. I'll stitch it up myself." That freaked *him* out. Wearing a surgical mask, he left for the hospital, where he was immediately ushered into a sterile examining room. He came home two hours later, tetanus shot administered, and wounds bandaged—none requiring stitches. He had only the highest praise for the medical staff.

Two days after Larry's ER visit, friends were anxiously awaiting the birth of their first grandchild. The impending delivery was made more stressful as it was uncertain whether their son could be in attendance: some New York City hospitals were not allowing any partners in the delivery room. Everyone was relieved to learn that he could accompany his wife during delivery, but the planned birth was still fraught with worry. If either of the expectant parents had symptoms, would she have to deliver alone? And would she or the baby contract the virus while in the hospital? Thankfully, the baby was born without complications. The proud grandmother sent me a picture taken in the hospital of the father dressed head to toe in scrubs and a surgical mask gingerly holding the swaddled baby in his gloved hands. All that was visible were the father's proud eyes.

The coronavirus has taken much from us, but the inability to congregate, to be together, to hug one another in times of joy or sadness, is the most painful. In normal times, we come together to celebrate the birth of a baby, to support ill friends, to say goodbye to a beloved friend or relative. During this time of a "new normal," grandparents cannot hold their newborn grandchild. Friends and family cannot celebrate birthdays, weddings, and *bar and bat mitzvahs*. High school and college students cannot celebrate graduations. Jews cannot gather around a huge table or meet in a large room to hold a seder. Most tragically, family and friends cannot even help those who lost a loved one to grieve, to offer hugs and a human touch.

One day, in the unforeseeable future, the corona virus will be behind us. We will gather together and hug each other tightly and even plant kisses on each other's cheeks that are wet with tears of joy. We will hold our friends and family not only in our hearts but also in our arms.

On Friday, March 20, for the first time since serving Congregation Beth Shalom, the rabbi did not conduct Shabbat services in Kissimmee. The synagogue, like thankfully churches, mosques, and other religious meeting places were closed due to the pandemic. In an email sent to the entire congregation, the rabbi suggested the following: "At 8:00 p.m. when we would all prefer to be together in the sanctuary, let's do two things that are emblematic of the worship service: recite the *Sh'ma* and *Mi Shebeirach* prayers."

Larry and I could not be together with other members of our congregation. Instead, we set the table with white linens and good china and crystal wine glasses. We lit the *Shabbat* candles, said *Kiddish*, and ate the delicious warm challah I had made from scratch. We recited the *Sh'ma.* Then we prayed for all of those—too many to even count— in need of healing.

Mi shebeirach imoteinu, m'kor ha-bra-cha l'avoteinu
Bless those in need of healing with r'fu-a sh'lei-ma
The renewal of body, the renewal of spirit,
And let us say Amen.
Stay well. Stay safe. Stay home.

April 16, 2020

Chapter Five

Hemingway, House Cats, And Hyper-Allergies

E rnest Hemingway loved cats. I knew the minute I walked into his former house in Key West in February 2020, just weeks before the pandemic closed down the world. Despite the beautiful day and the open windows, the smell of felines permeated every room. Our tour guide Doug introduced us to Gloria Swanson, Rudolf Valentino, and Betty Grable, three of the forty plus six-toed cats that roamed the grounds. All were descendants of his first polydactyly cat, Snow White.

I also love cats. Our family always had one or two when I was growing up. We had to give away two Siamese beauties when we realized that they were using the space under the clawfoot tub in our bathroom as a litter box. Most of the time, however, the cats stayed with us until they disappeared. My favorites were Romeo and Juliet, the former renamed Rebishka when "he" delivered a litter of kittens on my bed while I was sleeping in it.

When our children were young, we were given a stray that we named Fluffy. She died of feline leukemia three years later. By this time, it was obvious that Larry was allergic. This didn't stop me from adopting two more. "The children miss Fluffy," I told Larry.

Salty, the orange tiger, was more loving than his misnamed aloof sister Cuddles, a calico. He especially loved Larry, who sneezed and sniffled every time Salty sat on his lap.

One evening, before Larry left for a synagogue board meeting, he gave me an ultimatum: find a new home for Salty or find a new husband.

Soon after he left, I got a phone call from my friend Diane, who is even more allergic than Larry.

"The kids brought home a stray kitten," she said. "Could you please take it in until you can find it a home?" I couldn't say no.

Larry came home that night to THREE cats. Fortunately, I didn't need to find a new husband. A co-worker immediately adopted Pumpkin, and a few days later another friend adopted Salty. We were back to a one-cat household.

To no one's surprise, Larry became Cuddles' favorite human. The two of them often played cat ball. Larry would roll up a piece of aluminum foil, skid it across the floor, and Cuddles would bat it around the house. When she was fourteen years old, our beautiful cat disappeared one night and never returned. A friend consoled me with the suggestion that Cuddles was fox food. We found cat balls for months. Ten years later, while in the process of installing a new dishwasher, we found no less than twenty of them in the briefly emptied space.

By this time, we realized that all of us were allergic to cat dander, but I never have lost my love for them. When I visit a house with cats, I can't wait to pet them and hear that wonderful purr. So, at the Hemingway House, I petted each one that got within arms' reach.

At one point, I also loved Ernest Hemingway, so much that I completed an independent study on him and his writing in my senior year at University at Albany. *The Sun Also Rises, Farewell to Arms, Old Man and the Sea*—I admired his sparse style, his characters, and his complex search for the masculine ideal. I was, as I have shared with readers before, young, naive, sometimes clueless.

It was not until many years later that my opinion of the author changed. Reading his novels and other material about Hemingway from a more mature eye, I saw more clearly the man behind the myth—a narcissistic, heavy drinking male chauvinist. As Bernice Kert stated in *The Hemingway Women,* Hemingway could not truly sustain any of his four marriages. "Married domesticity may have seemed to him the desirable culmination of romantic love," said Kert, "but sooner or later he became bored and restless, critical and bullying."

His relationship with his third wife, the American journalist Martha Gellhorn, clearly demonstrated these characteristics. Resentful of her long absences as she pursued international stories, Hemingway protested, "Are you a war correspondent or a wife in my bed?" The final straw for Gellhorn (and mine!) was when she learned that Hemingway had convinced Charles Cobaugh, her editor at *Collier* magazine, to send **him** to the European front instead of his wife. In her excellent novel *Love and Ruins*, Paula MacLean describes Gellhorn's reaction to the betrayal. "You could have gone to any magazine in the world, absolutely any of them. I didn't know you had such a cruel streak in you." Gellhorn found another—albeit more dangerous—way to the front and divorced him soon after.

Hemingway also has been accused of being anti-Semitic. As Mary Dearborn writes in a 2017 article in the *Forward*, the author's letters were laced with "nasty remarks about Jews." She states that in his first novel *The Sun Also Rises,* his character Robert Cohn is described as an obnoxious individual, a "*kike*" and a "rich Jew." Although some critics have given his writing as expressing the "fashionable anti-Semitism of the 1920s," I now find his treatment of Jews in his novels to be abhorrent.

Should I stop reading Hemingway's novels? No. If I boycotted every classic that contain anti-Semitic references, I would have to shelf huge chunks of English literature, including Shakespeare, Nathanial Hawthorne, and Charles Dickens. Even Phillip Roth has been accused of perpetuating Jewish stereotypes in his literature. The list gets longer if I add on further classics that demonstrate other racial and ethnic slurs.

So, as we muddle our way through the pandemic, I will continue to read Hemingway and other renowned authors with a little less enthusiasm and a little more critical eye. And maybe, in the future, I will have on my lap while reading, a lovely Balinese—or another of the seven "hypoallergenic" cat breeds known to produce fewer allergens. In a tip of the hat to my favorite Hemingway wife, I will name my new love Marty. *Take that, Ernest!*

Originally published January 20, 2020; Updated for this book.

Chapter Six

Top Ten Pandemic Survival Tips

L arry and I have been sheltering in place since March 10, leaving our house only for daily exercise and essential outings. We consider ourselves fortunate. We still get our pension checks and our social security. Even though we are considered more vulnerable because of our age, we are—so far—not dealing personally with COVID-19 illness. We are not trying to balance working from our kitchen table while home schooling our children. We have few appointments and fewer deadlines.

These past few weeks have given us a perspective as to what is important in our lives. Once we have the required essentials such as toilet paper, masks, disinfectants/hand sanitizers, and a well-stocked kitchen, what do we deem necessary to get through the COVID-19 pandemic? Here is my own Top Ten List.

1. Real News

Larry and I have gotten a newspaper delivered to our doorstep since we bought our first house in 1976. When we moved to Florida, we immediately subscribed to the *Orlando Sentinel*. I can't imagine my morning coffee without the news, and our life would be a little emptier without the comics and puzzles. In the same way, I look forward to getting *The Jewish World* in my mailbox every two weeks to get the Jewish perspective. We have on-line subscriptions to the *Washington Post*, the *New York Times*, and the *New Yorker*. They were invaluable to me before the pandemic but even more important now.

2. Exercise

Now that the pickleball courts, the pools, and the gym are all shuttered, Larry and I alternate between riding our bikes and taking long walks every morning. We get some fresh air and have the opportunity to wave and greet friends and neighbors.

3.   A Sarong

If we were up north, we would probably be living in sweatshirts and pants. As Florida's temperatures rarely go below 75 degrees, I love my sarongs. They are comfortable and no-fuss and keep the laundry to a minimum.

4.   A Kindle

Through the miracle of modern technology, I have access to a public library with just a few clicks of the computer. If the book isn't available, I place a hold and get an email telling me when it is available. Best reads so far: *The Giver of Stars* by JoJo Moyes and *She Said: Breaking the Sexual Harassment Story* that helped ignite a movement by New York Times writers Jodi Kantor and Megan Twohey.

5.   Amazon Prime and Netflix

We can't go to the movies, and every live performance has been cancelled. But we finally have the time to watch all those series that were on our to-do list. Larry and I can recommend *Unorthodox, Schitt$ Creek*, and *Bomb Girls***.** I also have *The Marvelous Mrs. Maisel* and *The Crown* in my queue.

6.   My Writing

Our calendars are pretty bare, but I still have my deadline for the articles I write for *The Jewish World***.** Writing gives me a purpose. Recently, my articles about COVID-19 have helped me cope and put things in perspective. Once the article is published, I put it onto my blog, *www.theregoesmyheart.me,* and my Facebook pages. I love the sense of accomplishment I get from completing an article. I also love the feedback I get from those who follow me.

7.   Dinner

With all the restaurants closed and take-out options few and far between in our area, dinner is a main event. We even have a nightly happy hour with homemade hors d'oeuvres. Every Friday, we have a Shabbat meal complete with a *Kiddish,* candle lighting, and a homemade challah. Ironically, along with toilet paper and hand sanitizer, yeast has also been in short supply. I finally bit the bullet and overpaid for a pound of yeast on Amazon, so I don't have to worry about finding it in our supermarket. I make three or four loaves a week and drop off one or two to neighbors who need some cheering up.

8.   Our Lanai

Our lanai, which looks out on a small pond and a heavily wooded area, is our favorite place in our home. We are entertained by Florida wildlife, including a resident alligator, an assortment of birds, and a rare bobcat sighting. It is where Larry and I spend afternoons reading books and doing puzzles. The lanai table is my office, where I do my writing. And it is where we eat dinner each evening.

9. Video Chats

The hardest part of our quarantined life is not being with family and friends. Our trip to California to see our grandson and our summer plans for Colorado are on indefinite hold. At least four times a week, we FaceTime with our almost five-year-old granddaughter. We read her books, tell her stories, and watch her play. We usually end the call with her "reading" a book she has memorized to us. Holding our grandson is impossible, but my son and daughter-in-law are good about setting up the camera so we can watch him for a chunk of time. We Skype with Larry's side of the family on Sunday morning and Zoom with my side of the family on Monday night.

10. Our Support System

Absolutely nothing that I listed above would be possible without those who continue to work. People still deliver our newspaper, our mail, our packages we have ordered on-line. In our community, people still mow our lawns and pick up our trash and recyclables. Those who work in essential businesses—pharmacies, supermarkets, gas stations—still fill prescriptions, stock shelves, and run cash registers. A delivery service drops our groceries on our front porch. Most importantly, our first responders and all those who work in the medical field put their own lives on the line every day to try to save the lives of family members and friends who have been infected. I am so grateful to every one of them. We can best show our appreciation by doing whatever we can to prevent further spread of this epidemic. Stay safe. Stay healthy. Stay home.

April 30, 2022

Chapter Seven

Corny

One of the advantages in living in our community in Florida is the abundance of wildlife that surrounds us. In the past week, we have seen otters frolic near our pond, crows attack a red-tail hawk, and an osprey dive into the pond to catch a fish. Just tonight, as I was writing this story, two deer munched on grass near the pond.

In one of my more harrowing moments, I barely missed hitting a male deer who decided to dash across the road in front of my bicycle. I thankfully stopped in time and watched two adults and one fawn continue their stampede. None of this week's wildlife scenes, however, can compare with our encounter with a not-so-wild animal that briefly came into our lives.

As Larry and I were finishing up one of our long walks around Solivita, we saw a friend of Larry's from pickleball standing beside her bike and staring at the curb. As we got closer, a tiny ball of fur crossed the road, an animal so small that it took us a minute to realize that it was a kitten. We watched it dart behind some bushes in the front of a neighbor's yard. After a few tries, I found it trembling under the shrubbery.

Larry and I knew that we couldn't just leave it on its own. It would die of starvation or become an alligator's dinner. We also knew we couldn't keep it. Although we had had cats while our children were living at home, we had come to the realization that both of us were allergic. We had to find a new home.

I picked it up, wrapped it in the bandana that I had been using as an emergency face mask, and started walking the half mile home. It took me less than a minute to name the stray "Corny" for the coronavirus.

While I gently held Corny and tried to reassure the trembling animal that it was safe, Larry called friends who we knew loved animals. Kerry the dog walker. Jane the dog sitter. Doug and Barb the cat lovers. Teri who volunteers at a "cat cafe" where one can have coffee and pastries while playing with adoptable cats. In between the calls, we asked everyone whom we passed if they would like to adopt a kitten. No luck—yet.

When we got home, I placed a laundry basket with an old towel on the floor of the garage and sat next to the trembling animal. I took a picture of Corny and posted it on the lost and found section of our community e-bulletin. My next call was to a local veterinarian, who was not encouraging. He said that the kitten was one of many who were dumped in Solivita by outsiders and probably was carrying fleas, feline AIDS, and/or feline leukemia. He bluntly suggested that we call the county animal control so the stray could be picked up and—probably—put down. The Polk County contact initially provided some optimism: the shelter would take it in and try to find it a home if and only if it was weaned as they did not provide bottle feeding.

After several more phone calls, we connected with Brenda and Marty, devoted cat lovers who spend part of each year working at Best Friends Animal Society in Kaleb, Utah. The organization is leading a national effort of "No Kill by 2025." They also shared with us some sobering statistics confirmed by an article in the *Lakeland Ledger*: Polk County has a 50% kill rate for the animals brought to their shelter. That ranks them first in the state and tenth in the entire country. Corny wouldn't have a chance! They directed us to a woman in our community who is involved in Helping Paws, a local network whose mission is to rescue cats and find them homes. She was willing to take Corny, and the organization would ensure the cat visited a veterinarian for a check-up, shots, and neutering.

I quickly called animal control to cancel, but I was too late as the truck pulled up to our house soon after I hung up. We explained the situation, and the nice person who was to take Corny away said he was glad we found a home for the otherwise doomed animal.

As Larry drove, I held Corny, assuring the animal we were going to a safe place. Diane, the cat angel, took a quick look at Corny and immediately identified "it" as a "he." She thought Corny was less than six weeks old. Other than a few fleas and an eye issue, he appeared to be in good shape. She already was fostering a female cat with four kittens and was hoping Corny would be adopted by the mother cat. We gave Diane a contribution to cover the cost of the vet and said goodbye. The softie that I am, I shed a few tears as we drove home. From the time we first spotted the kitten until we returned home, only 90 minutes had passed.

The next morning, Diane left a message on our voice mail: the mother had accepted Corny. Diane texted us a picture of all six cats. The mother was nursing three of her kittens and Corny. A fourth kitten looked on with an expression that said, "Hey! Who is this grey fur ball that took my place?"

On a check-in a week later, Corny, whom Diane had renamed Snickers, was doing fine. "I overestimated his age," said Diane. "Based on his weight, he was less than four weeks old." While the other kittens were weaning themselves, Snickers had the mother cat all to himself.

Meanwhile, Diane shared with us her story as to how she became involved in Helping Paws. Like us, Diane and her family had a number of cats when they lived in their home outside of Boston and later outside of Orlando. When the last one passed away, Diane decided "No more pets!" Soon after that, Diane was diagnosed with cancer. After she recovered, she decided that she needed to do something to give back to the community. One night, she dreamed that a black and white cat showed up at her doorstep. The next morning, she found a calendar with a similar looking cat in her mailbox. And that day, a black and white cat **did** show up on her doorstep. Fifteen years later, Max is the "old man" in her home with two other cats as well as a string of over two hundred cats she has fostered over the years. We believed Corny had a bright future, and we had our happy ending.

Sadly, we were wrong. A week later, Diane called to tell us that Corny had stopped eating. On the way to a second veterinarian visit, he passed away.

As we celebrated *Shavuot*, the Jewish holiday celebrating the giving of the *Torah,* soon after we tried to help Corny, I could not help but think of the sixth commandment: Thou shall not murder. In such worrisome, sad times, I still am so glad that we had made the effort to rescue the little ball of grey fur.

To learn more about Best Friends Animal Society, go to
www.bestfriends.org.

May 14, 2020

Chapter Eight

What I Miss Most

What I miss most during the pandemic is certainty.

Yes, I know the old adage that says life changes on a dime, that you never know what will happen tomorrow. But now my life is filled with *too* many questions regarding the future. Will Larry or I contract COVID-19? And if we do, will we die? How about my children and grandchildren? What are their chances of getting the disease?

We know the guidelines. Practice social distancing. Wash your hands. Avoid touching your face. Wear a mask. But will that be enough? We have gone to stores three times since March 6. The first time was to Publix, during a "senior's only" hour. Huge mistake. The store was mobbed, most people were not wearing masks, the wait at the checkout was a minimum of thirty minutes. We switched to Instacart. Just last week, however, we ventured out to Publix and Lowes, donned in masks and gloves, for some targeted shopping. I would estimate 80% of the people and almost all the employees (except one young woman sorting produce) were wearing masks. Were we safe? Every time we are in a public place, we reset the clock to see if symptoms occur in the next fourteen days.

And the biggest uncertainty? When will this end? The first thing on the agenda will be to see our children and grandchildren. As we had done for the past five years, we had booked our plane flights and rentals in Colorado for six weeks. This week, we sadly cancelled all our plans. We have worked with our rental person so that we can use the condo at a future date. But when will that be? August? September? Next summer?

The pandemic has also put seeing our new grandson on hold indefinitely. Prior to his birth in March, we had made plans to fly out soon after his arrival and stay at a bed and breakfast a few blocks from their home. These plans were cancelled, as well as all plans to see them this summer in both Colorado and California.

My children have been wonderful about keeping in touch through video conferencing. Adam and Sarah often arrange the screen so that our grandson fills the picture. We have seen him poop, burp, yawn, sleep, and squirm. We have heard him cry and sigh and make what Adam calls his pterodactyl sounds. But we haven't held him. When will that day arrive? Our granddaughter, with the help of her parents, also checks in often. We talk, read, or tell stories to each other, and virtually bake chocolate chip cookies together. But—again the but—when will we be able to actually hug her and kiss her beautiful *punim,* that face with those big blue eyes and wonderful smile?

Of course, we are not alone in this pandemic. Everyone faces an uncertain future, whether it be as trivial as getting a haircut or a long-overdue hair color, or as critically important as having necessary surgery. For parents working from their kitchen tables, they daily juggle their workload and their childcare and even home schooling. Will daycare resume this summer? This fall? Next January? And should they even send them? For those working outside the home—especially those on the front lines— they wonder if they will bring the virus home with them. And for those who have been furloughed or— worse—lost their jobs, they wonder when they will be able to return to work. When they are, are the benefits of a paycheck worth the risk of also exposing themselves and/or their families to COVID-19? Now that Florida has eased restrictions, a beautician told her client that her husband is battling cancer. "If I go back to work, I may bring the virus home. Do I stay safe or have money for food, rent, and other necessities?"

As most of my friends are also grandparents, they speak of so many missed opportunities. A Mother's Day visit. A high school or college graduation. And even those who live close to their families must watch their grandchildren play from ten feet away or on the other side of the fence.

What is one of the saddest parts of the uncertainty are those whose loved ones are in assisted living or nursing homes. One friend shared with me the loss of a parent who passed away from what their children say is a broken heart when he realized that he could not see his family in the foreseeable future. Another friend is limited to FaceTime with his wife who, even though physically two miles away in memory care, could be on the other side of the moon. My friend Allison, a member of my writing group, has her 99-year-old mother in a medical crisis in Trinidad, and she can only call her siblings to get updates. There is one certainty: many people who do not survive will die without being surrounded by their family. And for many more, they will grieve alone.

Before COVID-19, life felt more certain. Or was it? "The pandemic has handed out a stark reminder that the idea of us humans ever having had a locus of control is a complete myth," Allison shared in a note to the other members of our writing group. "Now that's a different type of loss—thinking we've lost something that we never really had."

This morning's news carried a glimmer of hope. The manufacturer Moderna said that the first coronavirus vaccine to be tested in people appears to "be safe and able to stimulate an immune response." Testing, however, was limited to eight healthy volunteers ages 18 to 55. Will this be the answer? Or will several other possibilities in the queue turn out to be the answer? Meanwhile we wait and hope and deal as best we can with these troubling, uncertain times.

May 28, 2020

Chapter Nine

When you're chewing on life's gristle,
always look on the bright side of life.
Monty Python

Silver Linings

I f these were normal times, Larry and I would have already flown out to San Francisco to meet our new grandson. If these were normal times, I would be writing this column in Colorado, where we would have settled into a summer rental close to Julie, Sam, and our four-year-old granddaughter. These are NOT normal times! Because of COVID-19, Larry and I are staying in our home in Florida for the first time since we moved here five years ago.

The two of us are both disappointed, but we are finding silver linings. We are healthy, we are safe, we are in a community that offers walking trails and swimming pools. We have discovered tree-lined streets, serene ponds, and quiet trails that we had not previously explored.

And we have re-discovered each other. We have never in our 46 years of marriage spent this much time together, and we are loving it. We walk or bike together almost every morning and then cool off in one of the neighborhood pools. In the afternoon, we sit on the lanai where we work on crossword puzzles and read books. After dinner, we play three games of Yahtzee (I won the championship in May; as of this writing, Larry is in the lead for June.) Then we settle onto our couch to watch shows on Amazon Prime or Netflix. In some ways, I feel as if we are on some type of extended honeymoon.

Many of our friends, like Larry and me, are fortunate enough to be retired and not dealing with health or financial issues. They have shared with me how sheltering in place has resulted in hidden blessings.

My cousins Ruthie and Yaacov Kiflawi, who live in Washington State, have found joy in their own surroundings. They spend hours on their deck, which overlooks the Little Spokane River. Teri Chaves, who would normally be up and out of her home at 9 a.m., now sleeps in and then takes a leisurely walk. She then enjoys her morning coffee on her screened-in porch while watching the abundant Florida wildlife.

Teri is also using this time for intellectual pursuits and learning. In anticipation of a 2021 post COVID-19 30th anniversary trip to Italy with her husband Mike, Teri is learning Italian with the help of a phone app. Susan Hoff-Haynes is learning Spanish with the same app and has also taken several Great Courses. Michelle Moriya has audited free on-line courses from several prestigious universities, including Harvard, Yale, and Princeton.

Others are testing out their green thumb. Sarah Rubin designated a corner of her lanai for an herb garden; Susan sent me pictures of her raised garden beds behind her home in Upstate New York. Virginia Allain, who is compiling her family's genealogy research, is also working on establishing roots in the soil by planting her 2020 Pandemic Victory Garden. "It serves as an affirmation that I intend to be around for months to come despite this virus," Virginia wrote in her blog *Finding My Mom.*

Candace Thompson stated that the months in quarantine have been the best months of her life, giving her an appreciation for little things. "A simple ride in the car really brings me joy now where it would've been nothing more than something else to do prior to the pandemic." In what she calls a "true sense of agency and empowerment," she planned ahead of the curve by stocking up on foods, creating reading and movie lists, subscribing to streaming services, and downloading workout videos on YouTube. Since sheltering in place, Candace has also joined several community-based advocacy groups that hold Zoom discussions on topics including COVID-19, racism, and the upcoming elections.

Zoom and other collaborative technologies are being used to make closer connections with friends and family. Marilyn Tayler is using Zoom and FaceTime to connect with old friends and participate in advocacy groups.

For some families, the pandemic has meant even more time with their extended families. Since Pennsylvania's stay-at-home order, Howie and Sandie Vipler have stepped in as the full-time day care providers for their two granddaughters, ages 1 and 4. "Time—especially with our grandchildren—has become more precious since this virus has struck," said Howie.

The pandemic has also brought the-strangers-who-live-next-door together. Joy and Ross Aronson are enjoying sidewalk chats—while social distancing—with people in their community whom they had never met as they all take their daily walks. An animal lover, Joy was also pleased to meet up with people who were walking dogs that they had rescued from shelters, another positive result of sheltering in place.

In some cases, unexpected illnesses have resulted in life-saving interventions. While vacationing in South Carolina, Ira Smolowitz complained of COVID-19-like symptoms. His symptoms of dizziness and shortness of breath, he and his wife Judy soon learned, were signs of a heart attack. Emergency surgery, five days in ICU, and three months of virtual doctor visits later, Ira feels blessed to be on the road to recovery. Judy has been his rehab coach and number one cheerleader. "It's a tough time to have medical needs," said Judy, "but we made it."

In a similar situation, Richard Porter, a friend from Texas, had triple bypass on March 13. The day after he was released, Dallas issued a shelter in place order and the hospital that was to provide follow-up services closed its doors to non-COVID 19 patients. His wife Betsy, who spent her career as a nurse, willingly took over Richard's cardiac rehab. Neighbors helped by providing meals and dog walking services. On May 13, Rich celebrated 60 days of recovery by completing a 3.5-mile walk. "We saw the silver lining in the slowing down of our lives that helped in Rich's successful recovery," said Betsy.

Sunny Hersh rediscovered—"for the umpteenth time"—how much she respects and loves her family. Her husband Scott has been painting the house and cooking wonderful meals. Her children are doing an incredible job of balancing their parental and career responsibilities. Even though her attention span seems to be getting shorter and shorter, Sunny said she still "has enough bandwidth to dream about the future and appreciate all of the above!"

Others are creating their own silver lining scenarios. Becky and Mark Silverstein, who have cruised 47 times in the last 20 years, reimagined their shelter-in-place experience as SHIP (**Sh**elter-**I**n-**P**lace) life. Their bedroom is now their cabin, and their lanai is the balcony They watch television and listen to music in their "entertainment venue." They enjoy breakfast and lunch at the "buffet" at the kitchen counter and dinner at their dining room table.

Only one week into SHIP life, the Silversteins hit a proverbial iceberg. That first Friday, they dug into their weekly pre-Shabbat house cleaning, which included changing the sheets, cleaning the toilet, and "swabbing the decks." "We were rudely reminded that we are not just passengers," Becky said ruefully. "We also are serving as the crew."

Okay, not totally smooth sailing. But Becky and Mark, as many of us fortunate enough to be healthy and financially able to cruise safely through this pandemic, can always find a silver lining.

June 25, 2020

Chapter Ten

Black Lives Matter

In 1994, I attended, along with a number of my colleagues from the Capital District Educational Opportunity Center, an Office of Special Programs (OSP) conference in downstate New York. After the opening night's dinner, I wandered over to the vendors' tables that had been set up in an adjoining room. The items included many that reflected the African American population which OSP served: Kente cloths, African artwork, Maasai beaded bracelets.

I also saw books including *The Autobiography of Malcolm X* and *Black Like Me*. I stopped dead in my tracks, however, when I saw *The Secret Relationship Between Blacks and Jews*. A quick scan through the thin volume told me all I needed to know: it was a sickening, highly exaggerated claim that Jews had a disproportionately large role in the black slave trade relative to their numbers.

Livid, I raised my voice to the vendor. "How can you sell a book filled with anti-Semitic lies and garbage?" I demanded. "This is a New York state-run conference!"

The vendor told me it was his right to sell anything he wanted. I marched back into the dining room, found our EOC director, and expressed my anger. When he downplayed the situation, I blew up. "If you don't find a way to get rid of that book, I will walk out of this conference, get a bus home, and contact everyone I can in New York State to tell them that the OSP is condoning anti-Semitism," I said. "I won't stay here if that vendor remains under this roof!"

Seeing not only my rage but also my determination, the director brought me over to the woman who ran the conference. She said, "I will take care of it." The vendor wasn't asked to leave as I had hoped, but the book was no longer on his table—or any other table at that conference.

I later learned I was not alone in my reaction to the 1991 Nation of Islam publication. When Dr. Tony Martin, a black professor at Wellesley

College, assigned the book to his introductory African American history class soon after its 1991 publication, Jewish students protested, and four national Jewish groups recommended the professor's job status be reviewed. [He remained on staff as a controversial figure until his retirement in 2017.] Both the Simon Wiesenthal Center and the Anti-Defamation League of B'rith have published rebuttals comparing the book to "the most infamous works of antisemitic propaganda in the 20th century." Most importantly, the book's thesis has since been refuted by mainstream historians, including the American Historical Association.

I had forgotten about that incident for twenty-six years. But when I saw the video of George Floyd dying under the knee of a callous, arrogant white policeman on May 25, I felt that same rage—and more. And I understood the incredible anger and massive protests that followed. If I could be so vociferous about a book, African Americans, Caucasians, Asians—the entire world—had every right to say, "I've had enough. Black lives matter."

In the weeks that have followed Floyd's killing, I have become even more "woke." Through discussions with friends, participation in newly found groups on social justice, and through voracious reading of both books and articles on the topic, I have learned that my empathizing with those who are the victims of systemic racism falls deeply short of fully experiencing their pain and anguish. It is time for me to speak out with the same voracity for George Floyd and against 400 years of systemic racism in our country.

I have always felt that as a Jew I understood discrimination, racism, and prejudice. Hadn't I had students in my first teaching job draw swastikas around my picture in the school yearbook? Hadn't I been told that I was good at "wrangling a bargain" because I was Jewish? Hadn't I read hundreds of books and articles about the Spanish Inquisition and the Holocaust and attacks on Israel?

But I started to listen, actually listen, and reflected on my life as a privileged white person. When my son was home from college on his summer break, Adam used to go for his run at night to avoid the heat. I worried that he would be hit by a car. But I never had to worry that he, like Trayvon Martin, would be stalked and even killed because he was "in the wrong neighborhood."

I reflected on what my Upstate New York neighbors, a bi-racial couple, had experienced. Their son was pulled over by the police because he was driving his father's red sports car. The same young man was almost arrested when he was locking up his family's restaurant as the police thought he was breaking in.

The first week of the protests, I stopped by to chat with my Florida neighbor and just blurted out, "I am so sorry for all you have been through as a Black mother."

"I know you have a good heart, Marilyn," she told me. "But we've been fighting this battle for 400 years." One of her battles: When her family was living in Philadelphia, her son was asked to visit some of his white friends in their neighborhood. "I sat him down and told him no," she said. His being in that section of town was too dangerous for a young Black man.

My friend Mayra opened up to me about her life as a Hispanic woman married to Robin, a Black man. Her family wouldn't talk to them for years. Meanwhile, Robin, who had a highly successful position as a supervising editor for a major network, had been pulled over and slammed against walls more times than he could count as police had questioned why he was driving in his own affluent neighborhood. Another time, Robin and Mayra were guests at a large party of one of the network executives. Robin was talking to a co-worker close to the front door of the large home. Incoming guests assumed he was the hired help and kept handing them their coats and pocketbooks.

Another friend shared her story of how her husband Bill was the victim of road rage, an encounter that began on a toll road that ended just inside their community's security gates. The car with a white man at the wheel drove through a parallel gate, pulled along beside him, and cut him off. The man then jumped out of his car, berating Bill for passing him on the parkway and demanded to know why he was in the 55+ community "You obviously don't live here," he was told. The driver's wife, who was in the passenger seat, offered to get out their gun. Fortunately, the incident ended when Bill drove away. Because it was captured on Bill's dashboard camera, it is being investigated as a hate crime. But I know that his residency would never have been questioned if Bill were white.

I am somewhat ashamed to admit that before May 25, I didn't "get it." But I am trying to catch up. I feel like the demonstrator at a June 2020 Black Lives Matter protest in Bethel, Ohio, who held a sign reading, "I'm Sorry I'm Late. I Had a Lot To Learn." May the memory of George Floyd be a blessing to his family and our country. And may we all continue to learn and move forward to a more equitable world.

July 9, 2020

Chapter Eleven

Ah Abbotts!

How will I celebrate a milestone birthday during the pandemic? That hoped-for week away with my family is out. A party at my home is out. Heck! Larry and I can't even head to my favorite restaurant and indulge in a filet mignon and my free birthday brownie sundae. But there is a silver lining. An Abbott's frozen custard stand is less than 33 miles away from our Florida home!

The history of one of my culinary favorites began in 1902 when a young and enthusiastic Arthur Abbott traveled the Eastern seaboard with summer carnivals. He eventually found his way to Rochester, New York, where he opened a stand across the street from Charlotte Beach on the shores of Lake Ontario and near a bustling amusement park.

According to Abbott's website, as word of his frozen concoction spread, people lined up from morning to night. From his newfound success, Arthur was able to buy and train his own racehorses. When he struck it rich after his horse Blue Man won the Preakness, Arthur, then in his 70's, retired in 1957 and turned over his scoops to fellow frozen custard lovers Lenny and Tibby Schreiber.

For many years, Tibby's parents owned a *kosher* meat market in what used to be during the 1930s, the heart of the Jewish community on Joseph Avenue in Rochester. The franchise is now run by the Schreibers 'daughter Gail Drew and her family. To this day, Abbott's supports the Tibby Schreiber Scholarship at the Jewish Home of Rochester for the children of employees of the skilled nursing home who are heading off to college.

Brenden Drew grew up in the family business where he started taking out the trash and washing dishes. He now is responsible for business development and franchising. "Every day it is an honor and a privilege to help grow the family business," Brenden said. "Our family loves supporting our communities and making each one of our guests happy. So do each one of our local owners who truly live the brand."

It took the Shapiros a few more years to discover Abbott's. In the early 90s, Larry and Julie went to Western New York for a track and field competition. They spent the night before the race with Larry's sister and her husband, who live in Rochester. They grabbed dinner on Charlotte's Beach, followed by dessert at Abbott's.

Larry was hooked from the first lick of his chocolate almond cone and soon introduced the rest of us to it. Everyone who knows me knows how much I love ice cream. But Abbott's chocolate almond frozen custard is in a class by itself. The chocolate custard is rich and smooth and creamy and delicious. What makes it outstanding are the roughly chopped roasted almonds that are stuffed into the custard. As one reviewer on Yelp raved, "It is like sex in frozen form!"

Whenever we went to Rochester, we made sure Abbott's was on our agenda. Fortunately, as Adam spent four years at the University of Rochester, we had plenty of chances to make a stop when we were there.

Sometimes once was not enough. In 2003, Larry and I went to a wedding that was held in a church in Rochester. On the way to the reception, Larry and I stopped at Abbott's for a pre-dinner cone. The next day, we went with the bride's parents to another Abbott's for a second helping. They knew how much we loved this stuff. When Larry had surgery on a torn ACL a couple of years later, they had the company ship out a couple of quarts packed in dry ice to him. He graciously shared it with me.

At this point, we thought Abbott's was only located in Rochester. In 2012, however, Larry and I were strolling down Fifth Avenue in Naples, Florida, when Larry began running down the street. "Come on! Come on! I have a surprise for you!" And there in front of us was an Abbott's frozen custard! Yep! Time for another chocolate almond cone.

The Naples franchise closed. Thankfully, another one of Larry's sisters spends their winters in Vero Beach, and every time we visit her and her husband, we hit Abbott's. They don't even have to be there. We celebrated Larry's 70th birthday by going to a beach farther down the coast and stopping at Abbott's on the way home.

Vero Beach is 100 miles away, not conducive to regular visits. And we don't get to Rochester often. So imagine our joy in discovering that an Abbott's opened in Winter Garden, only 33 miles up the road. We celebrated Father's Day 2020 with our first visit. It was almost as wonderful as we imagined, but we think they didn't hear our request for chocolate ALMOND, as we realized halfway through our cones that the familiar crunch was missing. Two days later, we had to get a bicycle tire fixed, and we were only 16 miles away from Abbott's. So, what is a thirty-two-mile round trip detour for the love of Abbott's? And this time we not only got plenty of almonds, but the size small was bigger than the previous Sunday's medium. Heaven!

We made our third trip up a couple of weeks later. Another bicycle tire blew, so we took another delicious detour. I am sure we will squeeze in another visit before my Labor Day weekend birthday. We are running out of bike tires, but we can find another reason.

When we make our trip up for my birthday cone, I will pack a cooler and plenty of ice, and we will bring extra home, including a quart for friends in our community who previously lived in Rochester. It may not be the celebration for which I hoped to kick off my eighth decade. But it's a sweet start!

August 6, 2020

Chapter Twelve

Hair-Raising Pandemic Tales

With all that has been happening in the world since February, the discussion of hair grooming seems to take up a great deal of time and space.

Six weeks after our life went into lockdown, Larry was looking more and more like Bernie Sanders. Trips to the barber were not an option, so he purchased a set of electric hair clippers through the internet. Larry could easily get the front and sides, but I was responsible for the "back forty." As I held the buzzing clippers in my shaking hands, visions of a *Big Bang Theory* episode in which Penny accidentally shaved a chunk out of Sheldon's hair flashed in front of my eyes. Fortunately, the clippers were fairly idiot proof. Five minutes later, the job was done. Larry looked more like himself.

Larry, along with many of his friends, have resorted to do-it-yourself grooming. Others have used this time to grow beards and ponytails. In our retirement community, grayer and balder versions of their long haired, bearded Sixties self are a badge of honor.

For my women friends, it is not so much a matter of length as a matter of color. More and more crowns betrayed the grey that years of Clairol had covered. The big question was not, "When will this pandemic end?" No, it was replaced by the more looming question: "Should I go natural?" When restrictions lifted in June, most women ran back to their hairdressers, begging them to do their magic. A few, however, used this opportunity to allow nature to take its course. One of my friends even consulted "a Silver Foxy" Facebook page for the best look.

Along with a number of less desirable traits, I did inherit my mother's genes when it came to hair color. Frances Cohen maintained her dark hair into her seventies. One of her favorite stories was a conversation her hairdresser had with another client. "I want the same color that Fran uses," said the fifty-something from her perch in front of the mirror. "What Fran has does not come in a bottle," said the hairdresser. Just before the pandemic, I decided to stop highlighting my hair and was surprised to see that my natural brown color had little to no gray. I questioned my sanity for the blonde-that-sometimes-looked-grey treatments I had done for years. Meanwhile, my friends just kept saying how lucky I was that I had not spent all the time and money they had themselves expended over the decades to change their grey.

In the meantime, another hair-raising adventure was happening in San Francisco. My grandson was born in March 2020 with a head of fine brown hair. One month later, he lost all the hair on top, which matched his father's own male pattern baldness. Unlike Adam, however, my grandson soon recouped the hair on top but lost it on the sides. At five months, he now sports a beautiful brown mohawk. This entire tonsilatory adventure is now captured in a series of pictures chronicly the ups and downs of our grandson's hair length.

My grandson may not care about the way his hair looks, but that is not the case for my five-year-old granddaughter. Two weeks ago, after not getting more than a trim in six months, she asked her mother to cut her hair "short like Abigail," a character from *Spirit*, her favorite animated show. Julie was hesitant as the last attempt at a shorter style resulted in a meltdown. But apparently it made all the difference when it was my granddaughter's choice. Julie texted her relief soon after she laid down the scissors. "I cut it once, and she made me cut it again even shorter. She's very happy!" Following the text was a picture of my granddaughter sitting in a laundry basket with a huge smile. It was a perfect haircut.

Less than twelve hours later, we heard the familiar ding of Julie's text message. "Well, crap!" she wrote. "My daughter loved her haircut so much and was so excited that she snuck in her room and cut more off. It was so short on one side I had to shape it into short bob/pixie cut. No pictures available as she is in tears right now."

The tears continued the next morning through breakfast and through a sad walk to pre-school. After a twenty-minute discussion on the building's steps, my granddaughter was finally ready to show her face and bob. Unbeknownst to Julie at the time, my son-in-law Sam promised a trip to the toy store after he picked her up that night. The now short-haired cutie returned home clutching a "wish list" unicorn that thankfully ended further tears.

A day later, we FaceTimed with my Colorado family and made sure to tell my granddaughter how much we loved her short hair. When she commented that it was "too short," we reassured her that her hair, unlike her *Zayde's* and her Uncle Adam's, DOES grow back.

Yes, between buzz cuts and bald spots and unplanned bobs, I will always remember all the hair-raising adventures from this pandemic.

August 20, 2020

Chapter Thirteen

Happy Birthday

H appy Birthday to the World! Happy Birthday to me! Happy Birthday to *The Jewish World*, a bi-weekly subscription-based newspaper in upstate New York.

I was born on Labor Day, September 3, 1950. As my mother's doctor had a noon golf date, my mom accommodated his wishes and delivered me at 9 a.m. How appropriate!

The Jewish World came along 15 years later. Inspired by Jewish community leaders with the idea that a newspaper would strengthen the community, Sam Clevenson published the first issue of *The Jewish World* before *Rosh Hashanah* on September 23, 1965. He believed it would help unify the Jewish communities of Albany, Schenectady, Troy, and the surrounding area of upstate New York. After his passing in 2008, his children Laurie and James ("Jim") took the helm.

The Jewish World offers so much to its readership. The bi-weekly not only covers local religious events but also covers a wide range of local, national, and international news that impacts our Jewish community. It is also a valuable source for happenings in the world of art and culture.

My personal connection to *The Jewish World* began in 2013. While at a *Hadassah* special events dinner, I visited the office, then located in Schenectady, to speak to Jim Clevenson. In my pre-retirement life, I had worked in public relations as both a volunteer and as part of my job at the Capital District Educational Opportunity Center, a division of Hudson Valley Community college. Jim asked if I would be interested in writing articles for the paper, but I countered with an offer to write personal columns based on my many years as an Upstate New York Jew. The first article, "There Goes My Heart," was published on August 15, 2013. Laurie and Jim must have liked it. Over the last seven years, I have had nearly 150 articles published in Sam Clevenson's brainchild.

Sam Clevenson edited the paper with Laurie's help from 1980 until his death at age 90 in 2008. His wife Pearl remained in their home in Schenectady until February 2011, when she died at 93. She was active in her synagogue, joined a bat mitzvah class when she was 60, and supported many philanthropic enterprises.

Laurie had worked in New York State government and in the restaurant business in Arizona before joining *The Jewish World.* She worked closely with her father, following the major events in the news cycles, becoming familiar with community leaders, monitoring Middle East politics, visiting Israel, editing and laying out the entire paper.

After graduating from SUNY-Binghamton in 1977 with a degree in philosophy, Jim edited *Kite,* the Clevensons' weekly arts newspaper. From 1980 to 1994, he served as general manager of the family's printing business, World Printing. He then ran World Media, a printing brokerage which specialized in academic newspapers and retail marketing projects.

James and Laurie have carried forward their father's legacy, redefining the paper's role in the community and developing an innovative business model. They are packing the paper with more local news and have added a dynamic web site and weekly e-newsletter to expand the readership. The Clevensons' are building on *The Jewish World's* role as a pillar of the Jewish community in Albany, Schenectady, Rensselaer, and Saratoga counties. They are cultivating new readers in the Berkshires, Hudson Valley, and the Catskills.

The Jewish World's audience is well-educated, economically viable and discerning, with a thirst for knowledge in all areas affecting their lives and the lives of their families. They welcome the paper into their homes not only to learn about specific religious events but also to be apprised of happenings within the worlds of art, politics, and culture. They enjoy learning about lectures, foods, charity, social responsibility, films, travel, health issues, education, finance, history, and leisure. They are active, engaged and involved. A recent community survey found that, of those responding, 71% receive *The Jewish World.*

Along with a long swim and a huge Abbott's frozen custard, I will be celebrating my birthday by Zooming with family and friends around the world. I would like to use this birthday column to ask you, my *Jewish World* readers, to help me celebrate by taking out a subscription to this important paper.

September 15, 2020

Chapter Fourteen

High Holy Day Love Stories

In September 2021, our synagogue opened up its doors after several months of Zoom services. Rosh Hashanah would be celebrated in person with fellow congregants. It was a new year and a new normal. Celebrating the High Holy Days with family and friends, however, will always be a tradition that dates far back for the Shapiros.

In 1951, Larry's father Ernie, a World War II veteran, was called back into the US Army. Larry's mother Doris, along with Larry and Larry's older sister Anita, moved from Schuylerville, New York, to Syracuse, her hometown, to live with her mother Rose and brother Asher during Ernie's deployment.

Larry, who turned three shortly after their move, remembers riding the family coal truck with Asher and tagging along with Bubbe when she went to her card games. Relatives and friends filled the house, including mealtimes, as Bubbe was a wonderful and plentiful cook.

This was especially true during the Jewish holidays, a tradition that continued after Ernie returned home. Doris, Ernie, Anita, Larry, and later Marilyn and Carole would pile into the car before each holiday to share huge meals around a crammed dining room table in the flat on Jackson Street.

By the time Larry had completed his bar mitzvah, Bubbe Rose found making the huge dinners for the entire family for High Holidays too much work. Doris took over responsibility for not only the meals but hosting. Doris spent weeks preparing the food, and the table showed it. *Matzah* ball soup, chopped liver, brisket, chicken, *kishke*, potatoes, *kugels*, several vegetables, honey cakes—it was repeated on the evening before *Kol Nidre*, the opening service of *Yom Kippur*. Then Doris would outdo herself the next evening as we broke the fast.

The 1973 High Holiday season especially stands out for Larry and me. Larry and I met at a Jewish singles Purim party that March. We both knew fairly quickly that the connection we made over *hamantaschen* was special. We dated throughout the summer, and six months after our *Purim* meeting, we were both ready to commit. On a beautiful day Indian summer day Larry took me to a romantic overlook at the Saratoga National Battlefield. As he was about to pop the question, he got stung by a bee. Man plans; bees sting. Oh well! Larry felt terrible, but I was clueless.

Rosh Hashanah fell only a few days after the bee debacle. Larry and I turned down offers for a ride home from services. While walking home, Larry talked hypothetically about our future: where we would live and how many children we'd have. I finally kiddingly asked him if this was a proposal. "Soon," he said.

When we got to Larry's house, we said hello to the family who were about to sit down for dinner. Larry and I went into a bedroom to drop off Larry's *tallit* and my purse. Larry said, "Will you marry me?" I said "yes." We started to kiss when Corky, the Shapiro's wire-haired terrier, jumped up and licked my face.

As I wiped Corky's saliva from my lips, Larry and I made a pact: We would keep our engagement a secret until after the holidays. Larry's father's birthday was on Yom Kippur. We would announce our engagement at breakfast.

The next week went by slowly, especially for me, who wanted to shout our news from the rooftops. After Yom Kippur services ended, Larry and I called my parents to tell them of our engagement. We then sat around the Shapiro's large dining room table with Larry's family for the traditional bagels, lox, and cream-cheese-centered meal.

After the main meal, we brought out dessert and birthday cake. Ernie blew out the candles and opened a couple of presents. Then Larry announced that he, too, had a present.

"What?" said one of his sisters. "Another stupid tie?"

"No," said Larry. "I am giving you a new daughter-in-law. Marilyn and I are engaged!" Everyone was thrilled. My now future father-in-law regarded it as one of his best presents ever.

Larry and I were married on September 8, 1974. A few weeks later, we attended High Holiday Services with Larry's family. After the last *shofar* blast, we went back to the Shapiros for their annual dinner, a tradition we maintained for almost twenty wonderful years.

When Larry's parents passed away only eight months apart in 1994, Larry and I hosted a Rosh Hashanah dinner at our home in Upstate New York for over twenty years until our move to Florida. Since our move so far from family, we have shared similar dinners with our friends at each other's homes and our breakfast with our fellow worshippers in the synagogue.

In October 2019, the High Holidays were about creating new memories and celebrating another romance. On a visit from his home in San Francisco that January, our usually reserved son told us that he was "kinda sorta seeing someone," a woman named Sarah whom he had taken out for Chinese food on December 25. As Larry and I had similarly experienced many years before, Sarah and Adam both knew quickly that the connection they had made over fortune cookies was special.

They dated throughout the winter, and only six months after their Asian dinner, they were both ready to commit. On a beautiful summer's evening, Adam took Sarah to a romantic overlook in Bernal Heights. Fortunately, no bees ruined their moment. Adam proposed. Sarah accepted. They were engaged!

Adam and Sarah were married in San Francisco in October 2019, on the same day as the 46th anniversary of the day Larry and I announced our engagement and what would have been Ernie's 100th birthday. Life has come full circle.

After the wedding, Larry and I remained in San Francisco to attend *Yom Kippur* services with Sarah, Adam, and Sarah's parents. After the last shofar blast, we went back to Sarah's parents' house for their annual breakfast, an event that included Sarah's Grandma Minnie's blintzes. "As we prepare for this time of reflection, renewal and rebooting of our spiritual lives," read their invitation, "we wish you *L'Shanah Tovah*. And we wished our newlyweds much health, love, and happiness.

September 19, 2019

Chapter Fifteen

Be RUTH-less

I will never forget where I was when I heard of Supreme Court Justice Ruth Bader Ginsburg's passing.

Larry and I were in front of our computer, chatting with our fellow Congregation Shalom Aleichem members before our Rosh Hashanah Zoom service was to begin. "Ruth Bader Ginsburg passed away," interjected a member who had just gotten the breaking news on his phone.

All chatter stopped. Then there were murmurs of "Oh No!" "Oh my God!"

I was devastated. My heart turned cold as I thought about what will happen to our Supreme Court if the current administration pushed through another conservative, anti-abortion, anti-gay rights individual. Larry saw my face and knew what I was thinking.

"It is Rosh Hashanah. For the next 24 hours, we take time to celebrate her life," he told me. "We will worry about its impact later."

Within hours of the announcement of her death Friday night, an outpouring of affection for the first Jewish woman appointed to the country's highest court had already begun. People spontaneously gathered on the front steps of the Supreme Court building, where she had served as a judge for 27 years, bearing candles and singing *Amazing Grace.* In other places in the country, crowds gathered to say *Kaddish,* to remember. At Central Synagogue in New York City on Rosh Hashanah morning, Rabbi Angela W. Buchdahl spoke at the virtual service from New York City's Central Synagogue. She honored Justice Ginsburg in an eloquent spoken and musical tribute to "a real *tzaddik*, a woman of justice." As pictures of the late Justice's life were displayed on the screen, the rabbi sang a beautiful rendition of Psalm 150 (Hallelujah / Praise God in His sanctuary) to the melody of Leonard Cohen's "Hallelujah." I cry every time I watch it.

In the days that followed, I read many Jewish interpretations of the timing of Justice Ginsburg's death. One *midrash* stated that Jews who die between Rosh Hashanah are fast-tracked to heaven as they are considered true *tzaddikim,* people of great righteousness. With the fact that Rosh Hashanah fell on *Shabbat* this year, the significance is deemed to be even greater.

As Jews and non-Jews celebrated her life, however, Republicans were already planning on her replacement. The body of this incredible woman was not even cold when Trump announced that he would name his pick. And his sycophants quickly fell into line. Forget that in 2016, President Obama's nomination of Merrick Garland was blocked by many of the same Republicans. "The American people should have a voice in the selection of their next Supreme Court Justice," stated Mitch McConnell in March 2016. "Therefore, [Justice Anthony Scalia's] vacancy should not be filled until we have a new president." This obviously did not hold true for the current administration.

What was even more disturbing to me was the president's attempt to besmirch her legacy. Clara Spera, Justice Ginsburg's granddaughter, asked her Bubbe in her last days if there was anything she wanted to say to the public that hadn't been said. Ginsburg stated, "My most fervent wish is that I will not be replaced until a new president is installed." The president came out and publicly suggested that the Democrats fabricated Justice Ginsburg's dying wish. "It sounds so beautiful," said the president in an interview on Fox and Friends, "but that sounds like a Schumer deal, or maybe Pelosi or Shifty Schiff." There is no limit to the depths of indecency this man can go.

Within a few days, Senator Mitt Romney signaled that he was on board with the Senate taking up a new Supreme Court nominee during the current election year, an announcement that almost ensures the president's pick will be confirmed. The news hit me as hard as November 9, 2015, when I learned that Donald J. Trump was to be our new president.

"I am so, so sad," I shared on my Facebook page. "Women's rights will be gone. The Affordable Care Act will be on the chopping block. The election may come down to the Conservative, Trump-leaning Supreme Court. Goodness knows what is next."

By their support of another Trump-appointed justice, Republicans have stolen the rights and protections of Americans, particularly those of women, immigrants, minorities, elderly, and other vulnerable populations. It may take a generation or more, but I hope someday my great-grandchildren will live in a country that defends rather than undermines its democratic principles. Our country will look back ruefully but with relief for having overcome this chapter in which Republicans were on the wrong side of history. They snatched power from the deserving and flattered themselves in the delusion that they helped those whom they were hurting.

Ruth Bader Ginsburg, a legal pioneer for gender equality and the second woman to serve on the Supreme Court, has died. The possibility of a Supreme Court with a conservative majority is becoming more of a certainty. Where do we go from here?

November 3 is coming quickly. Honor Ruth Bader Ginsburg. Keep hounding your representatives, even if many don't appear to care beyond their own self-interests. Work to get out the vote. Write postcards and letters. Participate in phone banks and texting sessions. On November 3, vote as if your life and the lives of your children and grandchildren depend on it. And on January 20, you can share my joy as we welcome a new, better day in America.

October 10, 2020

Chapter Sixteen

Measure For Measure

Hindus and Buddhists call it Karma; Germans call it *Schadenfreude.* But do Jews have an expression to express fate or to express pleasure derived by someone from another person's misfortune? The closest corresponding phrase is *"midah k'neged midah,"* measure for measure. It means one's actions and the way they affect the world will eventually come to that person in ways one might not necessarily expect.

In a 2017 *dracha,* Rabbi David Wolfe described two Biblical passages from *Bereishit* (Genesis) that demonstrate this concept. In the first passage, Jacob takes advantage of his father's age and blindness to fool Isaac into believing that he is his older twin Esau. As a result, he receives his older brother's birthright/blessing.

Years later, Jacob falls deeply in love with Rachel. Agreeing to work for seven years for her father Laban, Jacob finally joins his bride under the *chuppah.* When he wakes up from the wedding night, however, Jacob realizes that under that heavy veil was Leah, the older and less desirable of the sisters. Rabbi Wolfe then calls on a *midrash* to explain the aftermath. Understandably, Jacob is extremely upset and demands to know why Leah tricked him. Leah 's response was "You fooled your father into thinking you were your brother; I fooled you into thinking I was my sister." In other words, what goes around comes around.

Just past midnight, on Friday, October 2, President Donald Trump tweeted that he and the First Lady had tested positive for COVID-19. The president's diagnosis came after he spent months playing down the severity of the outbreak that has killed more than 215,000 in the United States and hours after insisting "the end of the pandemic is in sight." He has downplayed the virus again and again. More egregiously, this cavalier attitude has been passed on to his supporters. Republican leaders have incorporated this non-scientific approach into their politics, resulting in dismissing the need for masks and social distancing, opening up cities and states way before it was deemed safe by experts to do so, and touting the "success" of such operations that in truth do not exist.

After initially experiencing some of my own Schadenfreude, my Yom Kippur prayers of repentance kicked in. I sought out the high ground, which I saw in the Book of Proverbs: "If your enemy falls, do not exult; if he trips, let your heart not rejoice" So summoning up my best self, I hope that the president has a r*efuah sh 'leimah*, a complete recovery. I hope even more that this experience changes how he views COVID-19 and its impact on those not able to take a one-mile plane ride to the country's top hospital after experiencing "mild symptoms."

Larry and I have seen our lives upended, as have our extended family and our friends. Aborted trips. In-person visits replaced with FaceTime calls. Cancelled bar/bat mitzvahs, graduation parties, and weddings, Zoom funerals. Limited visits with relatives in nursing homes.

But what we have experienced is nothing compared to the physical, emotional, and financial impact it has on others. On March 31, 2020, my friend Kathy, who had returned from a cruise "under the weather," sent out a Facebook post that she was being admitted to the hospital for what she believed was bronchitis. Within two days, she was hooked up to a ventilator. Her brother Brian kept us informed daily on social media, describing Kathy's ordeal in ICU in which she almost died several times. When she was finally breathing on her own, she spent several more weeks in rehab. She returned home two weeks ago, only to be rushed back to the hospital for more surgery related to complications of COVID-19. As I said, I hope for the president's recovery, but I wish he could experience just a fraction of what Kathy has been through.

Kathy has survived, but at least seven people in our community have succumbed. In the Orlando, Florida, area, thousands have lost jobs as Disney and other theme parks, Central Florida's main employers, have seen low attendance. The ripple effect has closed many of our area's restaurants and other businesses.

So, I know I join many Americans who hope that the Rose Garden Debacle, which lead to innumerable cases of this fast-spreading disease, will result in policy changes from President Trump and his supporters. Will the federal government finally organize a national response? Will masks and social distancing be mandatory everywhere, even when the president and like-minded Republicans are in attendance? Will first responders be finally given all needed supplies, including personal protective equipment (PPE) and enough tests? And will all leaders take a harder look at returning to Phase 1 protocols?

Or maybe I am just dreaming. On Sunday, October 4, I watched in disbelief as news stations covered the president's commandeering of a motorcade to greet his supporters outside of Walter Reed Hospital. Let us put this ten-minute joy ride into perspective. Because of COVID-19, millions of us cannot see people we love. Because of COVID-19, thousands have had to lie in hospital beds with no contact with relatives. Because of COVID-19, many have DIED alone. But the president thought nothing of spending thousands of our taxpayer dollars to get the adulation he cravenly requires. And he thought nothing of the danger he put his secret service staff (who were subsequently put in quarantine) and others to pull off this publicity stunt. To use the words of a popular meme on the Internet: I don't wish this virus on anyone. I hope the president has a speedy recovery. And I hope he gets demolished at the ballot box. That will be for me *"midah k'neged midah,"* the most satisfying measure for measure possible.

October 8, 2020

Chapter Seventeen

Let's Hear It For The Girls

Victoria has a secret during the pandemic.

She is NOT wearing an underwire. And neither are many other women. Yes, we have expunged our Exquisite Forms, ousted our Olgas and wiped out our Warners. Instead, we have traded our confining, pokey attire for the comfort of sports bras, bralettes, or maybe even nothing! Not since the Sixties, when we were burning our Balis have women felt so liberated!

I conducted a highly scientific research study by posting the following question to my women friends on Facebook: "Have you liberated your girls since you've been sheltering in place/working from home?"

One friend wrote, "NEVER!" Others wished they could but were afraid of their "flapping in the wind." Many, however, have ditched their underwires for more comfortable underthings. Those who went full commando were positively gleeful. "I haven't worn one since quarantine time started, in or out of house," replied Becky. "Quite enjoying this and might have a hard time going back!" Bev wrote, "Best part of quarantine!"

I am retired, so maybe my casual lifestyle isn't a stretch. But you have had to live under a mushroom not to know that few people are dressing for success these days. It's not only our underwear that has changed. We have ditched constrictive clothing for yoga outfits, caftans, or pajamas.

We may put on more public clothes for our trips to the supermarket, and we may don nice clothes (at least from the waist up) for our Zoom sessions. Personally, I have said goodbye to restrictive clothes and said hello to sarongs. I purchased my first green wrap (also known as a *pareo* in Tahitian or a *shmatta* in Yiddish) in Jamaica to wrap around my bathing suit when heading to the resort beach. I now own over ten in different colors and fabrics. They are light, versatile, and perfect for Florida's heat and humidity. Larry has even purchased a men's mini version. Dinners on our lanai wouldn't be the same without our wearing strategically knotted wraps while listening to Radio Margaritaville on Sirius XM.

So here is the first mystery of this pandemic. Larry and I are obviously not putting much effort into our attire. So why are we doing so much laundry? We need to wash our exercise clothing after one use (you cannot swim, bike, or play pickleball in a sarong). And we do shed all clothes we have worn on one of our exciting outings to the supermarket and library.

But we still seem to be working our Whirlpool quite a bit. I have decided that the pandemic has brought out the "Happy Homemaker" in me. I am cooking and baking more. Coupled with our obsessiveness for hand washing, surface wiping, and sanitizing, I end up with piles of towels and cleaning rags.

And here is the second mystery of this pandemic. Somehow, when I do venture into my closet for something with a waistband, it appears that my clothes have shrunk. Again, using my highly scientific method of asking the question on Facebook, it seems that this phenomenon is widespread (especially in the hips and waist). Something alien must have taken up residence in my closet. Certainly, it isn't related to all our homemade meals! Or the glasses of wine in which we have been imbibing every day since

lockdown. Or binge watching *Schitt$ Creek* or *Outlander* or repeats of *The Big Bang Theory*. Or even worse, what is now known as the Covid Curve or Quarantine 15, which thankfully has not happened to me yet. I have left several messages with my pest control expert to see if he can exorcize this demon along with the occasional ghost ant infestation, but he hasn't responded.

Until then, I will rely on my sarong to keep me happy and stress free. Hopefully, when this pandemic is over, we may see a permanent change in our wardrobes. Those in cold climates can have their yoga outfits and sweatshirts. I will be stocking up on sarongs.

October 22, 2020

Chapter Eighteen

I Am Thankful. I Can Breathe

For the first time in four years, I can breathe.

On November 9, 2016, I couldn't. In the early morning hours, I had learned that Donald J. Trump, defying most odds, had been elected president of the United States. With a heavy heart, I attended our community's *Hadassah* fashion show luncheon. I saw my own dread reflected in the faces of my friends who, like I, were dressed in black.

At the beginning, I tried to accept the fact that a reality television star was leading our country. But my worst fears were soon met and surpassed as the months and years passed. His lies. His bullying. His infatuation with autocrats His refusal to disavow white supremacy. His hypocrisy. His dysfunctional family and his incompetent staff. His wanton disregard of every social and constitutional norm to further his own insatiable ego. I was literally and figuratively holding my breath.

I wasn't alone in my assessment. Democrats, then Independents, then many Republicans stepped forward in articles, books, interviews to expose the emperor's new clothes. A 10/10/2020 *Boston Globe* editorial best expressed my feelings regarding four years of Trump. "Can we go just one day without a hateful or terrifyingly ignorant statement, a disqualifying act, a gambit that eats away at our democracy?" Yvonne Abraham wrote. "Might it be possible to read a book before bed sometime, instead of doom scrolling into the wee hours to keep up with his latest abuses and cruelty?

Could we wake up just one morning without thinking: *Lord, what has he done now?"*

I vowed that I would fight back. I joined local community action groups that provided constructive outlets for political activism. My writing offered another way to express how the Trump presidency was impacting me, my family, our country. I was initially concerned about the selection of Joe Biden because of his age. His decency, sincerity, and experience converted me into a true believer. His choice of Kamala Harris, a Black/Asian woman, sealed the deal.

On Rosh Hashanah, further spurred on by the untimely death of Ruth Bader Ginsburg, I made a commitment to work especially hard over the following weeks to make sure Joe and Kamala were elected. Volunteering with various political groups, I wrote postcards, texted, called those identified by Democratic organizations as potential supporters. "Can we count on you to support Joe, Kamala, and Democrats down the ballot?" I asked again and again.

The weekend before Election Day, I volunteered as a poll greeter. "If you are voting Democratic, I can provide information on the amendments and the judges," I offered. Many shook their heads and walked away, but many others—especially the first-time voters—were grateful and enthusiastic. After they voted, several asked me to take their picture with their "I voted!" sticker while they held a Biden/Harris sign.

Tuesday, November 3, was a waiting game. I took a long swim, volunteered at our community's Democratic booth, and then came home and tried to keep busy. The first results felt like a repeat of 2016. Florida was one of the first to be called for Trump, with other solid red states following its lead. "He is going to win again!" I cried to Larry. "How is our country going to survive four more years?"

By the next morning, however, I had heeded Biden's message, "Be patient!" As more precincts across the country began reporting, I and fellow supporters were more hopeful and increasingly optimistic as the United States collectively held its breath.

On Saturday morning, I was sitting at my kitchen table after a long bike ride, watching the news to catch the latest update. At 11:24 a.m., "Breaking News: Stand by for CNN projection" flashed on my television screen.

"After four long tense days, we've reached a historic moment in this election," announced Wolf Blitzer.

"Larry!" I yelled. "Get in here! You need to see this!"

"...CNN projects Joseph R. Biden, Jr., elected the 46th president of the United States, winning the White House and denying President Trump a second term."

I screamed, jumped up and down, and punched the air with both fists. "Yes, yes, yes!" We hugged. Then I called my five-year-old granddaughter, who joined her parents in screaming with joy when I announced the news.

"I want you to know that today a decent man was elected president and a decent Black/Asian WOMAN was elected vice-president," I told our granddaughter "I hope you remember this moment for the rest of your life."

By 12:30, Larry and I had finished off a bottle of champagne. By the end of the day, we had been in touch via text, email, phone, and Zoom with jubilant family and friends from around the country and the world.

In between, as Larry took a break to watch a Syracuse football game, I stayed glued to the television as spontaneous celebrations erupted across the country. Champagne bottles popped, car horns blew, pots and pans and drums banged; masked revelers hugged. The last time I had seen such an outpouring of joy were scenes from V-Day and from the collapse of the Berlin Wall.

The celebration continued that evening as President-elect Biden spoke in front of a cheering crowd in his home state of Delaware. "I pledge to be a president who seeks not to divide but unify," he stated. "Who doesn't see red states and blue states, only sees the United States." Then he was joined by Vice-President-elect Harris in her suffragette-white pantsuit and their extended families.

At four a.m., I woke up with a start, afraid I had been imagining all that had happened on Saturday was a dream. Then I smiled, inhaled deeply, and, wrapping my arm around my husband, fell back to sleep.

We still have so much to do. As I write this, Trump still has not conceded and many Republicans are supporting his claims of voter fraud. COVID-19 numbers are on the rise, seriously impacting the economy and so much more. We face the senatorial run-off election in Georgia. And Biden will face a challenging term. But today we celebrated. Today we begin to heal as a country.

"Live your life in such a way that the entire planet doesn't dance in the street when you lose your job," a favorite retweet read.

You're fired, Donald Trump. The nightmare is over. I can breathe.

November 19, 2020

Chapter Nineteen

A Hallmark Hanukkah

E ven though the pandemic has altered our world, my husband Larry and I will still maintain many of our traditions this *Hanukkah*. Eating potato *latkes* with applesauce? Check! Lighting the *Hanukkiah* candles each night? Check! Betting on which candle lasts the longest? Check! Watching Hallmark Christmas movies? Check!

Wait! Hallmark Christmas movies? When did *that* become a tradition?

For as long as I can remember, I have watched Hallmark movies. For many years, the famous card company aired shows specific to the holidays—Thanksgiving, Christmas, and of course Valentine's Day. Each two-hour made-for-television episode touched my heart. Many were based on classic novels, such as *The Secret Garden* or *Sarah Big and Tall*. Others were originals, such as *What the Deaf Man Heard*. And as much as I loved the shows themselves, I especially enjoyed the tear-jerking commercials (Did you know you can Google them? Watch them with a box of Kleenex next to you!)

In 2001, after the major networks dropped the specials, the company launched The Hallmark Channel. Building on its many fans during the holidays, their Countdown to Christmas began in 2009, a promotion of 24/7-blast of cheer that is still running today. Cookie-cutter stories, many based loosely on more expensive big-screen movies, have been churned out at an amazingly fast rate, with 136 to date. That is a great deal of "Deck the Halls" and "Jingle Bells," their favorite songs as the movies are touted to be about the spirit of the season, not religion.

Even though Larry and I watched the movies frequently over the years, what sent me over the edge was November 2016, when the election results triggered such fear and anxiety that my doctor put me on Xanax. Dr. Larry suggested an additional remedy: Turn off MSNBC and tune into Hallmark. I was off the anxiety medication in less than three months, but I still have my weekly dose of sap and sugar.

If you have watched only one or two of the productions, you have pretty much seen them all. The Christmas plot falls into two categories. Plot One: A high powered business dynamo needs to learn the real meaning of life and that he/she can only find in a small idyllic town inhabited by incredibly cheerful people who despite their low-paying occupations (cupcake bakers, store clerks, and staff at a huge inn with no guests in sight except the small cast seem to be a favorite) still can afford enough Christmas decorations to cover EPCOT. Plot Two: A poor but kind woman finds out that the incredibly handsome mystery man she is dating is actually the king of a tiny but wealthy country named after a countertop (Cambria) or china pattern (Winshire). Just before the commercial twenty minutes before the show ends, a conflict based on a misunderstanding erupts. No worries! It will be resolved with a kiss two seconds before the snow starts and two minutes before the credits roll.

Up until this past year, Hallmark was all about white heterosexual Christians. People of color were only seen as the best friend or the minister who marries the happy couple. Gays and lesbians were never seen. This type casting was blown out of the water last December when the channel first aired then immediately pulled an advertisement for an event-planning site that featured two women kissing at the altar. Within hours of its removal, the incident was all over the news. Within days, the president resigned. Within weeks, scriptwriters began churning out stories in which gay, lesbian, and interracial romances are highlighted.

What has been missing are stories about Jewish couples. *Loving Leah* (2009) was the closest to a true Jewish romance when a non-observant Jewish bachelor feels compelled to marry his rabbi brother's widow to honor him via the ancient Jewish law of *yibbum* (levirate marriage*)*. The channel's attempts at celebrating Hanukkah, however, have been for me major fails. *Holiday Date,* one of three 2019 seasonal movies with a Jewish twist, involved Joel, a nice Jewish boy who pretends to be the boyfriend of Brittany, a nice *shiksa* from an idyll small town in Pennsylvania. "Hilarity" ensues when Joel, who grew up in New York City surrounded by at least one or two Christians, has no idea how to decorate a tree or make a right-sided gingerbread house or sing "Deck the Halls" (There is that song again!). My favorite moment is when, once the ruse is uncovered, Brittany's mother comes out of the kitchen holding a tray full of potato *latkes* and wearing an *Oy Vey* apron that she managed to find on the first night of Hanukkah in the town's only store. The plots of the other two, both involving interfaith romances, made *Holiday Date* look like *Casablanca*.

So why do I—along with many others who will not come out of the closet—love the shows? Simple. They are mindless, sweet, non-political, non-violent, and always guaranteed to result in a happy ending. I still cry every time King Maximillian and Allie embrace at the end of *A Crown for Christmas*. (Take that, you wicked Countess!) What held true for me in 2016 holds true in 2020. I need a break from COVID-19 and the elections and the transition. Grab the dreidel-shaped sugar cookies and hot chocolate. It's time for a Hallmark Christmas movie!

December 10, 2020

December 2022 Update: Hallmark has redeemed itself with *Eight Gifts of Hanukkah* (2021) and *Hanukkah on Rye* (2022), two fine movies with a (mostly) Jewish cast and great story lines!

Chapter Twenty

Family Of Stores

Before *23andme.com*, before genetic testing, before people poured through old census and courthouse records, our family had the best tool to connect with our ancestors—our parents, Fran and Bill Cohen.

Bill Cohen claimed he could sniff out family from ten feet or from 200 years away. According to Dad, we were related to Sir Moses Montefiore, a nineteenth century British financier and philanthropist; Stubby Kaye, American actor and comedian most famous for his role as Nicey Nicey in *Guys and Dolls;* and Madeline Kunin, the former governor of Vermont.

Dad didn't regard fame as the only criteria to be considered *mishpachah*—a Jewish family or social unit including close and distant relatives. If one had any Jewish connection, Dad would find some link no matter how obscure and embrace them as one of our own.

While my father connected, my mother, Frances Cohen, kept a more reliable account of our family tree that began in *shtetls* in Lithuania. Even into her nineties, my mother could share the convoluted genealogical history of our huge family. To add to the complexity, my father's grandfather married my mother's great-aunt, first cousins married first cousins; and two sisters from Vermont married two brothers from Toronto. That is not only a great deal of *mishpachah* but a great deal of *mishagas* (confusion)! My brother Jay would listen for hours, jotting down rough drafts of the convoluted branches on yellow legal pads that he filed away for a later date.

Jay also spent a great deal of time talking to our parents about the chain of family-run department stores that are intrinsically entwined into our family's history.

Pearl's Department Stores began in the early 1900s when our maternal great-uncle Paul Osovitz, unable to continue in the New York City sweat shops because of respiratory problems, was given money by his older sister Lillian to start a business in Vermont. Initially living with his uncle Archie Perelman in Burlington, Paul peddled wares he carried on his back throughout the rural parts of Vermont and Upstate New York. He saved enough to purchase a horse and cart. As his business grew, he invited his brother Joe to join him.

Paul and Joe opened their first store in Alburgh, Vermont. As people knew them as the "Perelman Boys," they chose the name of "Pearl's Department Store." To make the moniker even more accurate, they and most of the family changed their surname to Pearl. Joe eventually went back to New York City, but Paul built a small dynasty of over 20 stores, employing his relatives as managers and clerks. Our father, Bill Cohen, was one of those relatives, spending most of his life managing one of Uncle Paul's stores in Keeseville, New York.

By the late 1980s, however, big-box stores and highway systems like the Northway (I-87) rang the death knell for small-town family-run businesses. Pearl's closed its last store in 1988, only remembered through those who worked or shopped there and dusty records.

In 2015 Jay, retired and always a lover of minutia and trivia, began researching the history of each of the stores and the families involved. He Googled the internet for news stories, advertisements, and pictures. He contacted historians in the stores' towns. He reached out to the descendants of the relatives that managed or worked in Paul's stores. He then expanded his research to include stores and businesses owned by mishpachah that were not connected to Pearl's, including paternal relatives and my in-laws, who owned Shapiros of Schuylerville in Upstate New York.

Jay incorporated all his findings into a website he called *A Family of Stores*. "If you grew up in upstate New York (a.k.a. the North Country) or in northern Vermont anywhere from the 1930s through the 1980s, you probably remember a Pearl's Department Store in your hometown," Jay wrote on the site's home page. "You went there with your mom or your friends. You bought your Wrangler jeans and your school clothes or a Christmas gift. A Pearl's store was there before the Kmarts, Ames, Walmarts and the Northway."

The ongoing project, which Jay called a labor of love, also drew on his interest in genealogy. His two sons began hounding him. "Learning about

Pearl's is fine," they said. "But when are you going to pull out all those yellow legal pads you have stuffed in a drawer and create a family tree for posterity?" It took a pandemic to motivate Jay to dig them out.

Early in the COVID-19 lockdown, my three siblings and I connected with our paternal first cousins through weekly Zoom sessions. As we continued to shelter in place, our group of seven expanded to include over 22 cousins, their spouses, and even their children.

Each meeting was consumed by the question, "How are we all related?" Jay, who had screen-shared his *A Family of Stores* website, offered to pull it all together.

Using a template from *www.ancestry.com,* Mom's notes, his website, and updated information he gathered from the Tuesday Zooms, Jay meticulously created the framework of a family tree that documents both paternal and maternal sides of our ever-expanding family. When finished, it will include everyone from Moses Montifiore (Dad was right, as he was about Stubby Kaye and Madeline Kunin) to my nine-month-old grandson, a span of over 200 years. Thanks to Jay's efforts, we not only know our roots but also our far-flung branches.

Why don't we all submit our DNA to one of the popular ancestry sites to learn more? Two reasons. First, our entire family history goes back to the shtetl in Eastern Europe. Those of us who have had tests done show us as 98% Ashkenazi. No surprises there. The second reason is that—well—we have more relatives than we can handle! Jay said that he expects to connect the family tree to over 1000 people.

What if we finally cave in, send a sample of our saliva to a testing site, and find even more? Bring them on! After all, we are Bill and Fran Cohen's children. And we love our family…all of them!

December 17, 2020

Chapter Twenty-One

Wintering Through the Pandemic

In her book, *Wintering: The Power of Rest and Retreat in Difficult Times*, British writer Katherine May recounts her own "sad" time where she was forced to hunker down after a family illness. "Wintering brings about some of the most profound and insightful moments of our human experience," she writes, "and wisdom resides in those who have wintered."

We are all "wintering" now through this pandemic. As we welcome good news with the rollout of the vaccines, we also grieve for those we have lost, those who remain ill, and all of us who have had our lives upended. But there WILL be a spring. I am not sure if I ever want to go back to the phrenetic pace of our previous life.

My whole life has always been about filling up my calendar. I thought this would change once I retired to Florida, but the last five years have been even busier. My days—and in many cases Larry's as well—were filled with concerts and theater subscriptions and annual Disney passes and movies and dinners out. I scheduled so many events that neither Larry nor I could keep up, resulting in revelations of upcoming plans mere hours before they occurred. "You were going to tell me about this WHEN?" Larry asked, as he dressed quickly to get to an afternoon tribute band concert being held in our 55+ community. "Sorry, sweetheart," I responded as I quickly threw on some makeup. "I thought our tickets were for the evening show!"

Our lives were also filled with trips to visit our children as well as to see places on our bucket list. When we weren't away or running around to our innumerable commitments, we also enjoyed visits from friends and relatives. We refer to it as "The Tourist Season," where our sunny home in

Florida looked much more enticing than the snow and ice-covered homes, they tolerate February through April.

That life as we knew it drastically changed in March.

Julie and her family had flown in from Colorado on March 7, 2020, for a week, just as COVID-19 cases were beginning to spike. We stayed in a rented cottage on Indian Rocks Beach, celebrated the long-distance birth of our grandson on March 8, and enjoyed the sunshine. We felt safe on the sparsely populated beach. Once we got back to our home, however, we cancelled our plans to visit Disney World and prepared all our meals at home.

On Saturday, as Julie's husband Sam packed up their rental car for the trip to the airport, Julie pleaded with us to shelter in place until this was over. "Stay home, Mom and Dad," she begged. "This is really serious."

Despite her entreaties, Larry and I were still debating whether to attend our community theater group's production of *Deathtrap*. "This will be our last foray for a while," I reasoned. "We should support our friends who put so much time into preparing."

One hour before we were to leave, Adam called from California. "If you promise not to go to the play," he told us, "we will spend the next hour Zooming with you so you can watch your six-day-old grandson." We complied. Outside of trips to doctors, the supermarket, and small, socially distanced outdoor meetings, we have kept our promise for the past nine months.

But maybe, for those of us fortunate enough to have survived 2020 without major physical and financial catastrophes, this year has been a break from our normal "Rush, Rush, Rush" routine. Larry and I have found a new rhythm that has given us respite in unexpected ways.

Each morning, we exercise, sometimes together (bikes, walks) and sometimes on our own (Larry's pickleball and my swims). After lunch, we spend a leisurely hour or two on the couch doing duplicated crossword puzzles, working silently until one or both of us say, "I need help!" I find time to write while Larry satisfies his passion for history and sports with the help of Google. After dinner, a shared affair, we watch a Netflix or Amazon movie and read. I say a prayer of gratitude every day that I am going through this difficult time with Larry, my soul mate and best friend.

We both have appreciated the power of online technology, allowing us to keep up with far-flung family and friends. Adam and his wife Sarah have kept up their part of the bargain, FaceTiming with us several times a week with the camera trained on our ten-month-old grandson. Although we have yet to hold him, we have at least been part of his life, watching him sleep and poop as an infant to seeing him experience applesauce for the first time, pop his first tooth and crawl backwards.

Thanks to his long, elaborate stories, our five-year-old granddaughter often checks in with Zayde. She asks him to retell the story of how Wicki Wolf was foiled again by the forest denizens, which include "good" wolves, moose, and even a visiting alligator who somehow survives the Colorado winters. Julie and her husband often share the screen. Frequent emailed pictures and videos of both grandchildren keep us further in touch.

True, there are times that I fear we have maxed out on Zoom. Synagogue services and board meetings. Book clubs and writing groups. Planned meetups with siblings and cousins and friends. But we still have much more down time that allows us to savor what we have rather than rush to taste something new. Although physically distanced, we have become more emotionally connected with the people for whom we care and even reconnected with those whom we lost touch in the frenzy of busier schedules.

As 2020 ends, I know I join millions who are glad this year is over. A popular meme summarizes those feelings: "2020. One Star. Very Bad. Would not recommend." I look forward to a healthier, happier, and more huggable 2021. But I also hope that I will retain the lessons I have learned as I experienced my own wintering.

January 7, 2021

Chapter Twenty-Two

"I can't keep silent, in light of how my country has changed her face.
Won't quit trying to remind her in her ears, I'll sing my cries
Until she opens her eyes."
Israeli poet Ehud Manor
as quoted by Nancy Pelosi, US House Speaker
1/13/2021

The Whole World Is Watching

O n Wednesday, January 6, I turned on the television to follow the United States Congress's certification of the election of Joseph Biden as our 46th president. I listened in anger as Donald J. Trump delivered an inflammatory speech to thousands of protesters, egging them on to "take back the steal." I watched in disgust as thousands of protesters, including one wearing a 'Camp Auschwitz' T-shirt began their march to the Capitol. And I watched in horror as the insurrectionists, brandishing Confederate flags, Nazi symbols, and pitchforks, breached the Capital. As members of Congress were evacuated, took cover on the Chamber floor, or hid in darkened offices, the rioters marched through the People's House, vandalizing offices, graffitiing doors, and leaving behind a trail of destruction.

After summoning Larry to come immediately to see what was playing out in real time, I texted my children. "Are you watching the news?

Protesters breached the Capital. National Guard being called in," I wrote. "The entire Congress is behind locked doors away from windows!"

"Mom," my daughter wrote back fifteen minutes later. "Everyone in the *world* is watching."

That was confirmed soon after when friends in England emailed me with just a subject line: "What the hell is going on?"

"Another day in Trump's America," I responded.

Yes, just another day that many of us saw coming. Since announcing his candidacy and targeting Mexicans as "rapists," Donald J. Trump has used his vitriolic rhetoric to disparage those who stood in his way and enflame those who supported him. In 2017, the president stated soon after the white supremacist protests in Charlottesville, Virginia, that there were "very fine people on both sides." His repeated inability to denounce neo-Nazis demonstrated to me that the lessons of World War II and the Holocaust meant nothing to him.

I also have been appalled by his comments directly targeting Jews. After the October 2019 massacre at the Tree of Life synagogue, Trump's initial reaction was to criticize the Pittsburg, Pennsylvania synagogue. "If there was an armed guard inside the temple," he said, "they would have been able to stop him." In August 2019, he accused American Jews of being "disloyal" to Israel by voting for Democrats. In December 2019, speaking at the Israeli American Council, he referred to the dual loyalty cliché and then went on to call Jews involved in real estate "brutal killers, not nice people at all." During the Republican convention, Mary Ann Mendoza was pulled from the event's line up after protests erupted regarding her promotion of anti-Semitic and QAnon conspiracy theories on her Twitter Feed.

His comments and policies have also impacted Latinos, Muslims, Blacks, Dreamers, Africans ("shit-hole countries"), and Asians ("kung fu" flu). Even the disabled—including those who suffered physical or emotional injuries as a result of their military service ("losers" and "suckers")—have been the target of the president's disrespect and scorn.

Meanwhile, since George Floyd's May 2020 murder, the United States has come face to face with its long history of systemic racism. The president has only fueled the flames. In June 2020, in a precursor to last week's violence, Trump and his administration ordered that law enforcement officers use tear gas and other riot control tactics to forcefully clear peaceful George Floyd protesters. The president then posed for photographers in what he perceived was his "law and order" stance that included his holding a Bible.

Despite his history of disrespect, cruelty, and divisiveness, between 21% and 30% of Jews (depending on poll used) still voted in November to give him another four years, citing what he and his administration had done for Israel (and their pocketbooks). In my opinion, they should be ashamed. Trump is an antithesis to every moral tenet of Judaism. He is a bully, a liar, a cheat, a womanizer, and a self-absorbed, unempathetic narcissist who has no respect for anyone who does not fawn over him—unless they are despots. And now he is being called a traitor to his country.

On January 13, 2021, the US House of Representatives voted to impeach Trump for a second time. Time will tell if the Senate tallies the 2/3's majority to convict him. It may take years to determine the political, financial, and legal fallout for him and his sycophants.

In the weeks leading up to the November election, while I was involved in getting out the vote against Trump, I purchased a sticker from the Jewish Democratic Council of America that read "Tikkun Olam: Repair the World. Defeat Donald Trump." He lost the election. Now he needs to lose all support and credence. Like *Haman*, may his name and legacy be drowned out by groggers, by history's judgement, and by the voices of all good people who recognize the damage he has done to our country and the world.

January 20, 2021

Chapter Twenty-Three

WWE 1, Marilyn 0

It was 8 a.m. Monday morning, and I was at our community pool to do my hour of swimming. I said hello to the one other person in the pool.

"Hi, Judy," I said. "How are you doing today?"

"Fine!" she responded. "But I wish I had come on Friday. I missed a big fight!"

"The f-f-ffight?" I asked hesitantly.

"Yes. I heard two people went at it when one of them wouldn't move out of a lane. Everyone is talking about it."

Crap! In a 55+ community that thrives on drama, it appears that my confrontation with a fellow swimmer had gone—if not viral—then aquatic!

Friday hadn't started out well. I had overslept and got to the pool late. Damn! That meant I would soon be competing with all the pool walkers and exercisers who usually were just starting their work-out as I was finishing up my swim.

Initially, everything was going smoothly. The sun was shining, the water was warm, and I glided down the lane line worry free. The walkers had arrived, but they were being respectful. I was, hopefully, doing the same. I watched for them as they came around the pool's sides and made sure to time my turns so we wouldn't collide, and I would adhere to social distancing rules.

With ten minutes to go, I caught through my goggles an anomaly among the usual sight of grey-haired ladies in skirted bathing suits and balding men in their knee-length trunks. A giant of a man—over six feet and two hundred and fifty pounds of pure muscle—waded into the water and stood in the middle of the lane next to me. He was clad in pair of short orange trunks that showed off a huge tattoo over his toned abs. His shaved head and gold earrings glistened in the sun as he started doing a stretch routine. Although not directly in my way, his leg-bending and arm swings felt too close.

After paddling past him a couple of times, I stopped mid-lap and asked politely, "Excuse me, but would you mind moving over a couple of feet. I only have six more laps to go, and I am afraid I might hit you."

"I am in the middle of the next lane," he said. "It shouldn't be a problem. Besides, you should be in the middle of the lane as well."

No matter that he could have been The Rock's brother. I was having a bad morning, and I lost it. "I have been swimming on this line for 50 minutes," I yelled. "It wouldn't hurt you to move two and a half &$#$%# feet so I can finish."

Done with my tirade, I kept swimming, making sure to splash vigorously every time I went past him. I was going to show him who was boss!

When I finished my laps, I climbed out of the pool. Taking off my cap, goggles, and fins, I began drying myself off with a towel. My friend Joyce, who had just arrived with her husband for her pool walk, greeted me.

"Good morning, Marilyn! How are you doing today?"

"I was fine until this $*#? got in my way during my laps."

"Who's that?" she asked.

I pointed to the aquatic Adonis.

"Adonis" began defending himself. "Hey! I didn't do anything! I try to be respectful to my elders! Everyone heard and saw what you did!"

"Him?" she exclaimed. "Why, that's Dom! He's Cherie's neighbor, and he is really nice!"

"Well, not today!" I grumbled.

At that moment, my friend Ann, who had overheard Joyce's comments, waded over to put in her two cents.

"Marilyn, that's Dom! He is really nice! He's Cherie's neighbor! I can't believe you yelled at him!"

Okay, he may have been a little too close, but I was wrong. I took a deep breath, put down my towel, and jumped back into the pool. By this point, mostly all the people in the pool were watching the drama between me and my sparring partner.

"Look. I want to apologize," I said. "My language and splashing were inappropriate. I just want to say I'm sorry."

"Hey, everyone has a bad day," he said. He held out his hand. "I'm Dom."

"I'm Marilyn," I said, grabbing his hand in return. "Nice to meet y...."

I dropped my hand. "Oh my God! Besides my husband, you are the first person I have touched since the lockdown!"

"Kinda like sex, isn't it?" commented Ann as the rest of the pool laughed.

I shared with him that I swim laps every Monday and Friday and always stick to the lines to give fellow lappers room. He shared with me that he went to the weight room almost every day and stretched in the pool afterwards.

"Yes, you LOOK like you work out!" I said. "You are—err—exceptionally built."

"I spent my life with WWE," he said. "I should be in good shape."

"WWE? As in World Wrestling Entertainment?" I gasped. "You mean I went up against a WWE wrester?"

"Yes, but I won't hurt you. As I said before, everyone has a bad day."

I climbed out of the pool and headed again to my towel when I stopped and turned around.

"Hey, Dom! I *do* take umbrage with one of your comments," I said. "You said you were respectful of your ELDERS. How old do you think I am?"

"I don't know," he said tactfully. "I'm 56."

"Okay, I *am* your elder. I turn 70 in two weeks."

"And you swim an hour each day?" he asked.

"I alternate it with 20-mile bike rides or 5-mile walks," I said proudly.

"Wow! I'm impressed!" he said. Wow! A WWE wrestler was impressed with me!

When I got home, I Googled Big Dom, which resulted in over in over 800,000 hits chronicling his history, which included several different story lines as both a good and bad guy. He even had a movie to his credit.

As a result, on that equally sunny Monday morning, I had to deal with my new notoriety. I shared the entire Friday Morning SmackDown episode with Judy, interrupted by her gales of laughter.

"I shouldn't have lost my temper," I told her. "I apologized! I am even going to bake a challah and drop it off at his house as a peace offering!"

So, I am now part of Solivita history. WWE One, Marilyn Zero. Maybe next time, I should take on someone my own size. Or—maybe next time I should just smile and move over to the middle of the lane.

February 2, 2021

Chapter Twenty-Four

Catch Me If You Can

Can a book change a life?

Our tenth-grade English class was deep into *The Scarlet Letter,* the classic by Nathanial Hawthorne. I was mesmerized not only by the writing and the story but also by its symbolism. Hester Prynne carried her shame on her chest every day: the bright red letter "A" which identified her as an adulterer. Things weren't bad enough in Puritan America without her not only to have to hold her beloved Pearl in her arms but also to have her shame emblazoned for all to see.

Our teacher, Mrs. Frances Clute, was a friend of my parents She and her husband John had spent time with our family, and she knew me well. One day, after class, Mrs. Clute asked me to stay a little longer. As the rest of my classmates dashed out the door for Mr. Kennedy's World History class, she pulled out a small book from one of her desk drawers.

"This is *Catcher in the Rye*, Marilyn," Mrs. Clute told me. "I know how much you love *The Scarlet Letter*. This is also a book that deals with symbolism. I am giving it to you with your promise not to share it with any of your classmates."

I was grateful for her trust. Even if I knew nothing about J. D. Salinger's 1951 classic, I knew she trusted me and saw in me the enthusiasm and the intelligence to handle its content and meaning.

I probably read it all that night, the whole story of Holden Caulfield, his depression, his flight from his private school, his trip to New York. I read how he wanted to save his sister Phoebe from any dangers that she would experience. I "got" the meaning of the "catcher in the rye," the person who wanted to always protect those whom he loved.

I also saw why Mrs. Clute had been furtive in her gift. The book had language that was certainly not in books usually selected by Keeseville Central School. I don't remember if it contained the "F" word, but it had other language and actions that were certainly not broadcast in our small upstate New York town. What made it great was the symbolism, the depth of the story behind the words.

I had already decided that I would be a teacher. After reading Salinger's classic, however, I knew I wanted to be an English teacher. I would spend my college years reading other classics, and then I would go on to teach others to love literature as much as I did. I followed that dream.

Looking back, I realize from my older eyes how shallow my understanding and appreciation of great literature was in college. There are classics that I read and hated, Moby Dick probably the most memorable. (I had to read it in one week. It was about a whale.)

In my first teaching job, I was assigned to share *Brave New World*, *1984*, and *Night* with juniors and seniors in a small-town school near Albany. I realized that not only did they not understand the books' meanings, but most of them couldn't even read. I had been a last-minute replacement for a man who decided in June to pursue his doctorate, and all the students had signed up to be in "The Cool Class with the Cool Teacher." I was not the cool teacher.

In the years that followed, I have tried and failed to read other classics, including *Les Misérables, Anna Karenina, War and Peace*, and *One Hundred Years of Solitude*. I missed the depth in so many books.

As I have every year, I have those four books on my "To Read" list. I probably will never get to them, preferring the New York Times best sellers and ones recommended by my bookish friends. But maybe, in honor of Mrs. Clute, I will take my copies of *Catcher in the Rye* and *The Scarlet Letter* down from my shelf. I will revisit my friendship with Holden Caulfield and Hester Prynne. And even though I know I still have a great deal to learn about literature and symbolism and the classics, I will accept that Mrs. Clute recognized that I had that spark in me. And for that I will be forever grateful.

February 2, 2021

Chapter Twenty-Five

Pandemic Purim Masks

W e're having a celebration for Purim," the president of our synagogue announced excitedly at the end of a recent Friday Shabbat services on Zoom. "We'll read the *Megillah*, watch some Purim music videos, and drink some wine. Can't wait to see your costumes!"

From our side of the computer screen, Larry and I exchanged looks. I had already found a Purim song by the Maccabeats and a presentation by Mayim Bialik that made me happier than reading the whole Megillah. After months of avoiding baking except for my weekly challahs, I had already decided that I would forget the diet and make hamantashen. But a costume? Maybe one of my numerous COVID-19 masks. As for costumes, the jury is still out.

My first memory of a Purim costume came when I was getting ready for the Purim festival for our North Country synagogue, Congregation Beth Shalom in Plattsburgh, New York, when I was about eleven years old. Along with the games and good food, there would be the yearly prizes for best costume. My mother had helped me cut out a huge replica of the Ten Commandments on pasteboard, and we put the Roman numeral numbers on with a thick marker. We created a beard out of black crepe paper. Once I put on a robe and a shmata (piece of cloth) cap on my head, I thought I was the best Moses in the history of the world. I just knew I was going to win the best costume award.

Unfortunately, the adult judges did not agree. I don't remember who won, but I remember it wasn't me. Being the rational, calm child that I was,

I had a meltdown in the car on the 30-minute ride home and continued to carry on when we got home. When I look back, I realize that my costume certainly wasn't original. In fact, every year, other parents had come up with the same idea. But I was crushed and swore off Purim costumes for twenty-two years.

On March 18, 1973, however, a group of my friends decided to go to a Purim party sponsored by Albany Jewish Singles. Those of you who know me, know that story. Although I did not wear a costume to the party, I did change into a long, flowered dress for an impromptu Purim *shpiel* that I, along with the six others in our assigned group, pulled together. In the skit, I was Esther to a cute guy named Larry Shapiro's Ahashuarus. He and I shared a hamantashen. By the end of the night, I knew that I would spend my life with him. As a friend with my camera captured at least a dozen pictures of the skit, we have a photo journal of those first minutes of our meeting. Meeting at a costume party on Purim was a wonderful way for Jews to meet. Over the years, however, I have often had to explain to my non-Jewish friends that Larry and I met at a **PUR**-im party, not a porn party.

Despite this memorably positive experience, it took 44 years for Larry and me to participate in another Purim event. A year after we moved into our active adult community in Florida, we were roped into performing in a Purim shpiel for the Shalom Club. Written and produced by Rochelle Willner, a long-time member of the club, the story was irreverent, campy, ridiculous, and fun!

Larry, who served as the emcee, pushed a Prairie Home Companion theme. He announced that the show was sponsored by the Hamantashen Council, who wants you to know "Hamantashen: It's Not Just for Purim anymore." I played a Vanna White wannabe, strutting across the stage with posters held over my head, announcing not only the number of the act but also cues as to when the audience was to boo for the villains and applaud for the heroes of the day. Other members of the social club played the more familiar roles—Esther, Ahashuarus, Mordechai, and Haman.

We were so bad, we were good. The audience loved us!

So why am I so against dressing up for Purim this year? First of all, we are having the celebration on Zoom, not at the synagogue. Do I want to put in all the time and effort to create a costume to wear in front of a computer?

More importantly, after wearing a mask on my face for the past twelve months, I find nothing exciting about purchasing a mask that does not provide COVID-19 protection. We have built up quite a collection to get us through the pandemic. Larry usually goes for solids, but I prefer a statement. One mask proclaims in big letters, "Because I care about you and me. Another is emblazoned with butterflies, my totem. My favorite is the one I purchased in memory of Ruth Bader Ginsburg, which has her portrait and one of her iconic quotes, "Fight for the things you care about."

If I wanted to get into the holiday spirit, Etsy, the online company, offers a variety of Purim themed COVID-19 masks, bearing pictures of hamantashen, masks, and Megillah scrolls. I can even invest in a personalized mask that proclaims "Quarantine Purim 2021. The Shapiro Family." Another simply states, "This is my Purim costume."

Next year, when we can hopefully celebrate without social distancing and without required masks, we may reconsider. This year, however, unless the president of our synagogue twists our arms a little, Larry and I will stick to the story, the songs, the hamantaschen, and maybe too much wine to get into the holiday spirit. *Chag Sameach!*

February 10, 2021

Chapter Twenty-Six

Biking for Ruth

When Ruth Bader Ginsburg, the legal pioneer for gender equality and the second woman to serve on the Supreme Court, died just before sundown on Rosh Hashanah, the Jewish new year, I shared the country's grief. What could I do to honor this gutsy, determined, badass woman? How could we continue her legacy in light of what we knew as the inevitability of her replacement with a woman who appeared to be the antithesis of whom the NPR called a "demure firebrand?"

Writing an article that was published by *The Jewish World* in October 2020 gave me comfort, but could I do more?

A few days later, a friend shared a link to a website that offered a way to honor the feminist icon. *Run for Ruth* was billed as a virtual event to "celebrate the life of Ruth Bader Ginsburg and her dedication to equality for all no matter where we are right now." Participants could run, jog, walk, or even swim to reach a total of 87 miles —the number that reflected RBG's age when she passed away. In addition, one could choose to donate to several charities earmarked as those representing RBG's legacy through their support of women's rights and empowerment.

The $29 entrance fee entitled each participant to a T-shirt with a picture of RBG wearing a crown; a digital race bib; and a finisher's medal. It also gave one access to a website which one could put in individual mileage, compare results with others involved, and even print out a virtual bib. The guidelines said that a minimum of 30% of registration proceeds would go to charity.

With visions of RBG smiling down from heaven, I sent in my online registration fee; donated money to Planned Parenthood, one of the charity options; and logged in for my first virtual entry–the 20-mile bike ride I took the day after Rosh Hashanah and two days after her passing.

No matter how or with whom I would put in the miles, I knew from Day One that I could not make my goal a paltry 87 miles. Since the pandemic had hit, I had swapped fitness classes for 7 a.m. swims in an outdoor pool and, accompanied by Larry, long walks and longer bike rides.

I had already put 1000 miles on my bike's cyclometer. Based on this knowledge, I set my personal goal for 870 miles by the January 31, 2021, deadline.

About four weeks and 230 miles later, I received the Run for Ruth race packet in the mail. The finisher's medal, a large metal medallion on a striped ribbon was pretty impressive but, in my eyes, pretty useless. I couldn't see when I would wear it and put it aside to give to my five-year-old granddaughter.

The bigger disappointment was the T-shirt. I had ordered an adult size large, but it fit like a child's medium. I couldn't even get it over my head. I gave it to my petite niece and found an even cooler RBG shirt on Etsey for myself.

Now that the focus was off the perks, it was time for me to put my pedal to the metal. Larry was a great biking partner, pumping air into our bike tires as needed, mapping out routes that avoided traffic, and scheduling hydration stops along the way.

By the middle of October, I was fully invested in what I now called my "Bike for Ruth." We were averaging over 19 miles a ride on our bikes and over 5 miles on our walks, along with one or two of my solo swims. Each day, I recorded my progress on the website and checked my results compared to fellow participants.

Amazingly, 1376 people ranging in age from 5 to 81 had signed up for the biking event. Predictably, many had not gone more than a few miles before dropping out. (Hope their T-shirts fit better than mine!). A couple of hundred had reached their goal of 87 and were done. But there were hundreds more who were still cycling along.

The results page not only gave names, miles, ages, hours expended, and hometown but it also listed rankings. And guess who was in the top 60 and climbing! Not only was I moving up the chart, but I was one of the oldest riders.

True, I had several factors in my favor. Others were dealing with snow and school and jobs and the pandemic—forget about hills! Mrs.-Retired-in-Flat-Florida could pedal and walk and even swim to her heart's content. And I had the spirit of RBG urging me on. I was getting closer and closer to my goal of 870.

One day, however, I noticed a fellow Floridian had slipped into the top 25. One entry. One day. 1067 miles. And this person was 75 years old! Impossible!

I decided the best way to handle what I considered an unacceptable entry was to ride more miles. I upped my personal goal from 870 to at least 1068.

By this time, it was mid-December, and Larry was getting concerned. Florida was experiencing its winter, and it had turned colder, windier, and even rainier. Could we speed this process up, maybe get done by January 1?

We both pulled the SmartWool gloves and Patagonia NanoPuff jackets we usually reserve for our trips to Colorado and soldiered on. I hit 870 on December 21 and 1068—Take That, 1067-in-One-Day—on January 4.

At this point, Larry, who was dealing with a shoulder injury, said that I was on my own. I cranked out another 300 miles and hit 1367 miles on the last day of the challenge. I finished in 10th place out of 1376, with the next person close to my age in 56th place.

I was waiting for the drum roll, or at least a shiny certificate in the mail. I would have waited for a long time. As you remember, I had gotten my "finisher's medal" two weeks into the race. And the black and white 5X7 online certificate listed in big letters my name and time expended: 109 plus hours. In tiny letters were my rank and the wrong age of 69. So, I created my own tribute that I have displayed on my refrigerator. It reads **Marilyn Shapiro. 10th Place. 1367 Miles. 70 Years Old.** Then I got back on my bike. After all, Ruth Bader Ginsburg's 88th birthday would have been March 15. And I am good for at least 880 or so miles before my pandemic pedaling finally comes to an end.

March 5, 2021

Chapter Twenty-Seven

Pandemic Passover Two

Passover did not completely pass over us in 2021. As we were only three weeks into the reality of the pandemic when we observed Passover last year, Larry and I had a small, quiet, seder for two. On March 27, we shared the traditional meal with members of our synagogue on Zoom.

Larry and I have been fortunate. As were our Hebrew ancestors, our family and circle of friends have been spared the "angel of death" in that we lost no one to this (God willing) once in a lifetime scourge. Friends who contracted the illness have survived, albeit with some lingering effects that we hope and pray will result in a *r'fuah sh'leimah*, a complete healing.

Despite my gratitude, I was feeling that more than Passover had passed us by. I know I share the feelings of so many others that we have lost a year of our lives. We not only missed out on life events—first birthday parties, bar/bat mitzvahs, weddings, graduations, funerals. We also had lost out on the small things: a restaurant dinner with friends; a movie or play, a live sporting event, a simple hug from a friend.

This feeling of ennui especially hit me when February arrived. Physically, I was doing fine. But emotionally, I felt sad and cold and dark. Would this pandemic ever end? Would we be able to travel to see our children and grandchildren this summer? When would the world begin to turn to normal?

In the middle of all this, I was working on my third book. *Fradel's Story,* a compilation of essays my mother had written in the last five years of her long life as well as articles I had written about both my parents and my siblings. After hours and hours of organizing, editing, and re-editing, what should have been a labor of love was turning into just labor. Of course, that put more pressure on me, something that I certainly didn't need in my emotionally depleted state.

On the third Saturday in February, I resumed my editing with "My Romance," my mother's description of her failed romances with men she had she dated while living and working in New York City in the 1930's. "The saying goes: You have to kiss many frogs until you meet your true love," she wrote. "Well, I knew many frogs."

All that changed when she was introduced to Bill Cohen, her brother and one of her cousin's co-workers in an Upstate New York clothing store. After a whirlwind three-month courtship, my father proposed over ice cream on February 14, 1940. "We had just seen *Gone With the Wind,*" Mom wrote. "Bill must have thought I was Scarlett O'Hara, and I must have thought he was Rhett Butler. I said yes."

Over the next six months, they maintained a long-distance romance, seeing each other infrequently but writing often. Mom had kept the letters in her dresser her entire life. "Where are those love letters now?" I thought. Then I remembered that they were in a metal box that held all my treasured correspondences, exactly where I had put them soon after her passing.

Even though I had known about them for at least sixty years, I had never actually read their love letters until that Saturday morning. My father spoke of his loneliness, his love (mixed in with some bad poetry), and his excitement about their pending marriage. My mom's letters shared some of his romantic sentiments, but she, always the practical one, also detailed the wedding preparations along with constant reminders for Bill to get the necessary medical tests before the August 20, 1940, ceremony.

After reading them all, I called my three siblings to share the emotional news of my find. That triggered more memories, more family stories. Laura reminisced how her eight-year-old self had found our parents' love letters and decided to play post office by delivering them to each of the mailboxes on our street. Jay remembered how, while living in that same Upstate New York house, he and a fellow five-year-old called the fire department to report a "blaze" so the two of them could get a firsthand look at the town's new fire engine. Bobbie retrieved another letter—the one my parents had written to her in 1977 when, as a recent college graduate, she was struggling to find a job.

After my phone calls, I went back to the kitchen table to resume work on my book, but I was no longer alone. I felt my parents 'strong presence surrounding me with encouragement to keep writing and with quiet assurance that—as they had done as members of the Greatest Generation—we too will survive this challenge.

On March 2, the tenth anniversary of my mother's passing, I sent my manuscript to my editor. Months of work were still ahead: more editing, picture placements, cover design. *Fradel's Story* was officially launched on

September 1, what would have been my mother's 104th birthday, with paperback and Kindle edition on Amazon.

Soon, I gave my house a thorough cleaning, made my chicken soup and matzah balls, poured Manischewitz wine over the chopped apples and nuts for the *charotzes*, and set our table for our Zoom seder. With all the recent good news on the medical front, I had faith that next year's seder would be a more crowded, joyous, affair. Thanks to the love and memories my parents and siblings have shared with me, my mood has changed to happy and warm and bright. Chag Sameach!

March 19, 2021

Chapter Twenty-Eight

Brown Thumbs and Public Gardens

If I were still living in Upstate New York, I would be thinking about planting my flower garden. Thinking—not planting—as it never seemed safe to put the annuals into the ground until Memorial Day weekend. Before I knew better, I had planted the fragile blooms too earlier and watched them die before they even rooted, hit by a late frost.

Not that I or any member of our family were known for our green thumbs. My family's track record for killing all but the hardiest plants dates back to August 1952, when we moved into our house in Keeseville, New York. While the inside of the house needed plenty of work, the previous owner, Laura Gardener (how appropriate!) kept a beautiful yard. A huge hedge of tiger lilies bordered the front of the house alongside a pristine lawn. In the back was a beautiful flower garden filled with fragrant phlox, lovely lilies of the valley, rose bushes, and a bird bath. At least that was what Laura and Jay, my two older siblings, remembered. By the time I first could recall the yard, it had already shown the neglect that my parents, who grew up in New York City apartments, had bestowed on Miss Gardener's labors. Sadly, it never regained its floricultural splendor while the Cohens lived there.

When I was around twelve, my father decided to put in a vegetable garden in our side yard. As with most of my father's projects, he was the idea man, and I was the unwilling implementer. We may have gotten some tomatoes that year, but by the next spring, grass was growing on the small plot and the experiment was over.

The idea man/implementer plan also worked for my father over twenty years later at the family cottage on Lake Champlain. One fine June morning, Dad showed me the roll of black mulch he had gotten on sale. "It's for my vegetable garden," my father announced. "Dad," I said. "You don't have a vegetable garden!" "I will soon," he told me, pointing to a tray of tomato and pepper plants and a hoe resting on a small patch of land next to the garage. "Start digging." For the rest of that summer during my weekend visits, I was like the Little Red Hen—planting, weeding, watering. Dad, however, was in charge of harvesting—proudly showing off "his" yield.

Meanwhile, Larry and I were already living our own "Better Homes and Gardens" experience. On a beautiful fall day in 1978, our realtor showed us what would be our future home. We liked the house but especially loved the large front yard and woods offering privacy in the back. When a squirrel ran across the plush lawn, we were sold. To this day, I swear that the owner had hidden behind a tree and released that rodent on purpose.

While Larry mowed, I planted. On or soon after Memorial Day, I would go to the local garden place and fill my car with red impatiens, begonias, salvia, and some coleus. I would clean up the rock garden on the side of our property and the area underneath the bushes along the front. I would dig and plant and water and weed until my back hurt. In a throwback to my making-mud-pies days, my favorite part was getting dirty, so dirty I often had to strip off the top layer of clothes in the garage before walking back into the house.

By the end of July, however, my enthusiasm had wilted with the humidity. I had grown tired of the heat, the bugs, the occasional snake, and the sight of almost everything I planted failing to thrive. I encountered success in only two areas: although the other annuals usually died an early death, the impatiens continued to bloom until the first frost. In addition, my hosta plants were the envy of the neighborhood, growing ridiculously big and needing separating every season until I had hosta growing around three sides of the house.

Any attempts at our growing a vegetable garden provided a bounty— not for us but for the wildlife and the insects. As had happened with my flowers, early June's enthusiasm was followed by August's failure-to-thrive. I learned that the vegetable stand on the corner of Grooms and Moe Roads was a tastier, less work-intensive alternative to hours in a garden to gather a few tomatoes and sad looking peppers.

After mowing lawns and raking leaves for over 35 years, Larry had turned over those jobs to our neighbor's son, who had started a lawn care business. Maybe it was time for me to hang up my gardening tools as well.

I found my escape when we relocated to Florida. Our community has a homeowner's association (HOA), whose fees include lawn care. I can leave all our landscaping chores to the wonderful people who descend on our property every Tuesday. After they mow our lawn and trim our bushes and trees, the workers munch on the cookies I gratefully place on their water cooler. A few extremely hardy potted plants on my lanai satisfy any urge I have to tempt fate to kill the un-killable.

Not all my neighbors have abandoned their gardening gloves. Many have turned their lanais into a virtual greenhouse with hundreds of potted plants, fountains, ponds, and even in one friend's home, a koi pond! For others, the lanai also serves as a vegetable garden, with shelves of herbs and large planters filled with tomatoes, a variety of peppers, and even eggplants. On our frequent walks, we have seen screened-in courtyards filled with raised beds filled with flowers and vegetables. And each month, one home sports a "Yard of the Month" sign in recognition of the owners 'dedication to their outdoor displays of flowers and landscaping.

Thank you, but no thanks. Outside of an occasional snip on a wayward bush, I am happy with our lawn service. If I want to see lush gardens, Larry and I can take a stroll in Bok Tower Gardens, a beautiful 250-acre garden and bird sanctuary in Lake Wales, only a short 40-minute drive away. Now that we are vaccinated, we will again be able to enjoy Epcot's annual International Flower and Garden Festival, complete with topiaries of our favorite Disney characters. Yep, this girl has switched out her hoe-hoe-hoes for a simpler life. Ho! Ho! Ho!

April 15, 2021

Chapter Twenty-Nine

Wasabi

Now that I am in my seventies, I am thrilled that I have acquired so much knowledge. My brain is a virtual 20-volume set of *World Book Encyclopedia* of both useful and not-so-useful information. Unfortunately, as a result, my ability to quickly retrieve a necessary fact sometimes fails.

Please understand. I am well aware that our memory is often no joking matter. I have too many dear friends and family who have cognitive disorders due to dementia and—heaven forbid!—Alzheimer's disease. A close relative struggles with recall because of a stroke she had five years ago. She has made tremendous strides since the first few days when she told us that she had been flown to the hospital in a "bulldozer." But I know she is embarrassed when she can't find a particular word. Those who love her keep reassuring her that it is not a big deal. We *all* have our moments when the words just won't come.

This inability is most seen when I need to recall someone's name. Sometimes I blame it on what I call a "You are out of context!" situation. The most memorable—and most embarrassing—incident of this phenomena occurred thirty years ago. Larry and I were in the lobby of Proctors, a theater venue in Schenectady, New York, when a man with a vaguely familiar face greeted us warmly. I looked at him and said, "I am so sorry! I forgot your name! How do you know us?"

"Marilyn, this is John Smith," Larry said. "He is our children's swim coach!"

"Oh, John," I said. "I am so sorry! I didn't recognize you with your clothes on!" Gulp!

As a classroom teacher, I took pride in knowing my students' names. Seating charts helped on the secondary high school level. When I taught adult education, however, enrollment was done on a rotating schedule. New students appeared every other Monday, and I didn't require seating charts.

Remembering names became a challenge, especially when my students had variations of the same name. When confronted with a Shaquana, Shaquilla, Shaquina, and Shakuntula in the same classroom, I struggled but triumphed in the end.

I have often used mnemonic devices to help. For example, I often see my neighbors Hope and Tony walking their golden retriever, Abby. At first stymied by our encounters, I now remember them with the phrase "Abby Hopes Tony will take him for a walk." Easy peasy!

I was so proud of myself for devising this trick, and I shared my method with them. Other times, it is best I keep my trick to myself. Two sisters who could almost pass as twins are often in my exercise class (when I was able to GO to exercise class! Damn pandemic!). I mixed up "Sally" and "Jane" for a while until I started paying this little mind game. Sally, who is married, wears a silver ring. The other sister, who one day shared with me day her unhappiness with her untoned arms, is remembered as Jiggling Jane. As long as Sally is wearing her wedding band and Jane is wearing a sleeveless top, I will never mix them up again!

This pandemic has had some limited benefits, and one is that we have an excuse when we forget a name. When someone greets me warmly, I reply, "I can't see your face behind the mask. Can you tell me who you are?" Great excuse, right?

I have also been bailed out by modern technology. Our synagogue meets on Zoom, and most participants, whom I already know, have their names displayed. I have little patience in any video conference settings for those who refuse to "get with the program." As far as I am concerned, they will be referred to "iPad 2" or "555-100-1111" until further notice.

This doesn't work in our neighborhood's Olympic-sized pool, where no masks—or name tags—are required. In those situations, I use the "55 plus community" excuse: "We live in Solivita where memory is just a memory," I say. "Please tell your name again."

I tried this approach recently, and the woman smiled and answered "Ingrid."

Then I had my own AHA moment! "Ingrid! I knew that! By the way, do you remember *my* name?"

"No," she answered sheepishly.

"Marilyn," I said. "It's Marilyn." And I resumed my swim, content with the fact that I was not alone in my affliction.

The loss of recall isn't limited to people. After twelve months without sushi, Larry and I purchased a tray of California rolls at the local Publix. That evening at dinner I was savoring each bite when I realized I forgot the name of the "green stuff."

"Larry, what is this called?"

"Wasabi," Larry answered.

94

Five minutes later, I had to ask again. "What did you say this green stuff is called, Larry?"

"Wah-**SAH**-bee," Larry said, drawing out the syllables.

The next morning, the first thing I thought about was the delicious California rolls we had eaten the night before. It took a long second to get the word for the "green stuff" out on my tongue.

Wasabi! Wasabi! Wasabi! I thought to myself.

An hour later, Larry and I were taking a walk when we saw another couple walking towards us.

"Quick!" Larry said. "His name is Bob. What is his wife's name?"

"Wasabi!" I quickly answered.

So, now when either Larry or I are in doubt, we just substitute our code word for our Failure to Remember: Wasabi. Wah-SAH-bee. For now, it's working.

April 29, 2021

Chapter Thirty

Fish Friday

F riday was fish day.

No, we weren't Catholic. Growing up in the Fifties, in a small predominantly Catholic town, fresh fish was often available on Friday. Looking back, I am not sure if it was truly fresh. Yes, Lake Champlain was three miles away, but I don't think local fishermen provided the fillets that lay on top of the ice in the Grand Union.

There was a second reason Friday was Fish Day. My father managed a department store, and Pearl's, along with the other stores in Keeseville, was open until 9 o'clock every Friday. Dad hated fish, so my mother would make some variety of it on that night. If it wasn't fresh, it is a frozen block or two that my mother defrosted, covered with breadcrumbs, and baked along with frozen French fries. When she wanted to save time, she heated up some Gorton's fish sticks.

Friday dinners were a contrast to our Monday-through-Thursday *Father Knows Best* routine. On those nights, Dad would come in the back door at 5:30 and immediately sit down at our Formica topped kitchen table. We children took our places, assigned after one night of our fighting who sat where.

"That's it!" Dad said. "Wherever you are sitting tonight will be your place from now on."

Dad sat at the head, his back to the radiator and the yellow linoleum tile on the wall. When she wasn't putting food on the table, Mom took her place at the foot, her back to the old white Kelvinator range cook stove with its double oven. Jay, the only son, sat to his left. Laura, the oldest daughter, took her place next to Jay. Bobbie, the youngest, sat to Dad's right. I sat in between Mom and Bobbie.

Dinner was usually chicken, potatoes and a vegetable that had been peeled off the waxed box and boiled in a pot on the stove until overcooked. Occasionally, we would have spaghetti with Ragu. Notice I didn't say *pasta*. In the 1950s, the only pasta available was macaroni for macaroni and cheese and regular old-fashioned spaghetti noodles. Who knew of such things as ziti or angel hair or cellentani?

Our dinners were usually over quickly. By 5:55, Dad had pushed himself away from the table. While the children dutifully moved to their bedrooms to do homework and Mom washed the dishes, Dad headed for the back room and the television set. The local news was followed by Huntley and Brinkley. The rest of the night was filled with *Perry Mason, Checkmate*, and other early television shows of his choosing. In those days before remotes, Dad would rely on us post-homework to change the station. This did serve an educational purpose: When Bobbie was in kindergarten, she was having difficulty learning her numbers. It was a eureka moment when our family realized that Bobbie had no problem changing the channels to Burlington's WCAX (Channel 3) and Plattsburg's station WPTZ (Channel 5).

The Friday late night closing provided another benefit to the four Cohen children. As we had no school the next night and Dad wasn't home to dictate what programs we watched, we ate our dinners on TV trays in front of our favorite programs. This included *The Mickey Mouse Club,* with our favorite Mouseketeers, Annette Funicello and Tommy Cole, and a little later, *The Flintstones.* By the 1960s, both my parents worked at the store, and I was old enough to look after Bobbie as we watched *Rawhide, The Wild Wild West*, and *Route 66.*

Where did synagogue fit into this picture, especially in our Reform congregation that only had Saturday morning services for bar mitzvahs? Mom finally got her driver's license in 1955, just before Bobbie was born. Driving the 30-mile round trip to Plattsburgh with four children in tow, especially in the winter, was out of the question. It was not until the mid-Sixties that Mom would make the trip with Bobbie and me. Although we all attended Hebrew school though Jay's bar mitzvah and all of our confirmations, a traditional Shabbat dinner with challah, candles, and a Kiddish cup was not even a consideration. Dad worked, and it was Fish Friday!

In fact, it wasn't until the pandemic that Larry and I started our own tradition. Last March, I became fully invested in baking challahs each Friday for ourselves and those friends whom we felt needed the comfort of a golden loaf straight out of the oven. We began lighting the Shabbat candles, pouring a glass of Manischewitz, and putting my cross-stitched challah cover over one of the warm loaves. How could we do all this and NOT set the table and prepare a special dinner, whether we were participating in our twice-monthly Zoom services or just enjoying a quiet sheltering-in-place meal at home?

As we and our friends are vaccinated, it is time to invite a couple or two or three to share this all with us. I look forward to carrying on this tradition with my children and grandchildren this summer. Yes, I have come a long way from Friday fish sticks in front of Annette Funicello and the Flintstones.

May 13, 2021

Chapter Thirty-One

Unmoored

S ince Larry and I have had our second COVID-19 shots, our pre-
pandemic life and its commitments are slowly resuming. We have
waded out into the unknown, first a toe into the water with outdoor
concerts and patio-only dining, then walking up to our knees with visits and
in-home dinners with vaccinated friends, then plunging in with indoor
restaurant dining and non-virtual club meetings. Recently, I was in a
restaurant with four friends when I realized I had walked in, sat down,
ordered, and hadn't thought of COVID-19 or even masks for a full half hour.
That, I say, is progress.

Then why am I feeling shaky? Uncertain? Unmoored?

Since March 2020, when the world shut down, my husband Larry and
I filled the empty hours that stretched in front of us with small gems. I finally
put together *Fradel's Story*, a collection of articles written by my mother
and about my family. We took long walks and longer bike rides through
unexplored areas of our community. We spent hours and hours on our lanai,
reading, doing puzzles, eating leisurely dinners, and watching the wildlife
in our pond. Each Friday, we celebrated Shabbat with candles and wine and
homemade challah. And we spent hours and hours on video conferencing
sessions with family, friends, our synagogue, and our clubs.

Now our calendars is filling up and overflowing. We have not yet given
up many of the activities that kept us going for sixteen months of isolation,
but we are also adding more and more semblances of our previous life. And
as what happens to me whenever I try to juggle too much, I begin dropping
balls. I missed a planned luncheon, showed up an hour late for a book club,

and completely forgot to call my brother and sister-in-law to wish them *mazel tov* on their fiftieth anniversary. For goodness sakes, I even failed to send in an article to *The Jewish World* for its last issue, something I had not done for years. Had I learned nothing from the pandemic?

Jodi Rudoren captured many of my feelings in a March 5, 2021, editorial in the *Forward* where she admitted that she didn't want to go back to the old normal. "This terrible, horrible very bad year of isolation has also had an abundance of silver linings," she wrote, "and I worry we'll snap back to our old ways without truly learning the lessons this crisis has brought."

So now, like Ms. Rudoren and many others, I am finding my own better normal. I don't want to give up some of the things I savored: the more leisurely life, our long dinners on the lanai with cold beer or coconut rum and (Diet) cokes or wine; the challah baking, the puzzles. On the other hand, I look forward to meeting friends for dinner and plays and indoor get-togethers, resuming exercise classes, and, most of all, traveling to see my family.

I am not alone in my feelings, as I found out on a Zoom meeting with my SOL Writers group. Ginny said that she feels as if she was emerging from a long illness, where stepping back into the world in her weakened state is difficult. "I feel untethered," she said. "It is as if I am floating around finding my center." Gail shared that she felt as if she were in a waiting room, in between her old life and her new normal.

Along with the difficulty of finding one's balance, there is still the specter of COVID-19 hanging over all of us. Although the SOL Writers have had both vaccines, each found that she still was a little too vigilant, a little too cautious, and most importantly, a little distrustful. When verbally accosted by a fellow shopper who demanded to know why she was still wearing a mask, Ginny avoided confrontation by calmly saying, "You care as much about what I think as I care about what you think." After losing what she feels has been a year of her life, Mary Ann said she no longer has the energy or patience to squander what remains of her time for idiots who still think that the virus was a hoax. Aya called them "energy vampires."

The reality of a resurgence has been felt by friends in England, who now are concerned of a virus variant from India that is more contagious. "Portugal opened up, and many people flew there for a vacation," they told us. "Then there was a spike in cases." Portugal's COVID-19 rates increased enough for England to revoke their green status, resulting in vacationers scrambling to return home before they faced a 14-day quarantine. Our friends are not optimistic about traveling for a long while.

In the States, there is more confidence, and Larry and I are ready for our next big step. We will soon be flying out to see Adam and Sarah and meet our grandson, who was born one day before San Francisco closed down. Then we head to Colorado, to spend time with our daughter, son-in-law, and beautiful granddaughter. Extra masks and hand sanitizer are already packed, along with gifts, warm layers for San Francisco summers and hiking clothes and boots for Rocky Mountain trails.

We know that COVID-19 and its aftermath will impact our visit. Outdoor concerts, farmers markets, and indoor plays and dinners are still "To Be Determined."

No matter, Larry and I will just be happy to finally be with our family and return to at least that piece of normalcy. We will take long walks along the ocean in San Francisco and long hikes in the woods in Colorado. Each Friday, we will sit down with them for *Shabbat* dinners with wine, candles, and freshly baked challah. Larry will find quiet moments to do puzzles and read. I will put the final touches on *Fradel's Story*. I will continue writing stories about living through the pandemic. And I will savor all that I learned as I move forward into our "new normal."

June 24, 2021

Chapter Thirty-Two

Farklempt: Part One

Yiddish may be one of the world's more obscure languages, but it has given us words which are no less than perfect. Someone may have nerve, but *chutzpah* reflects a shameless audacity that says it better. Being a good person is nice, but being a *mensch* brings that individual to a high level of honor, integrity, kindness, and admiration. One can complain, but when one *kvetches,* he also adds a layer of whining and fretting that truly captures the moment.

Another word that Yiddish does best is *farklempt,* overcome with emotion. I can count on one hand how many times I have ever needed to use this word or felt its power. The day I held our newborn son. Three years later, when I held our newborn daughter. And six years ago, when I laid eyes on my two-hour-old granddaughter. And now, I can use it again: When we were finally able to hold our grandson for the first time.

Our grandson was born in March 2020, a few days before the world closed down due to the pandemic. Larry and I were on Indian Rocks Beach, Florida, with Julie, and our granddaughter when Sarah went into labor in a San Francisco hospital. Adam announced their newborn's official arrival late that night via phone calls and texted pictures.

By the time Julie and her family flew back to Colorado later that week, the impact of COVID-19 on our lives exploded. We promised our children that we would stay safe and shelter in place. Larry and I had made reservations to fly out to California later in the month, but we had no choice but to cancel and wait until things improved. Little did we know at that the time that the wait would stretch out for over 15 months.

Thanks to social media, we got to see a great deal of our "San Francisco Kid." Adam and Sarah called frequently and focused the camera on our beautiful new grandchild so we could watch him sleeping, nursing, bathing. Then, as the months dragged on, we saw him learning to crawl, learning to walk, speaking his first words. But we were unable to hold him in our arms.

Larry and I tried to repeat certain rituals so that our grandchild would know us. Each time we connected, I would sing "The Wheels on the Bus." As the months progressed, I went beyond blinkers going left right stop and coins going clink clank clink. I introduced dogs barking and ducks quacking and pigs oinking and cows mooing, "Isn't that crazy?" I would ask him from 3000 miles away. "Ducks and pigs and cows on a bus?" Larry, meanwhile, would move two fingers against his lips and say, "Bu bu bu ba!"

By the time our plane landed in San Francisco in mid-June, Larry and I were beyond excited and also a little nervous. How would our grandson react to these two people whom he had only seen on a small screen? Would he cry? Turn away? After hugging Sarah until she couldn't breathe, Larry climbed in front of the Honda Civic with Sarah, and I tucked in the back next to our grandson's car seat. He looked at me as if to say, "Who is this lady?" I gently touched his arm, but he pulled it away. I softly started singing "The wheels on the bus go round and round, round and round, round and round..." His eyes got big, and he burst into a huge smile. And Larry? As soon as we got out of the car, Larry lifted him out of his car seat, held him with one arm, and with the other hand, did his "Bu bu bu ba! routine." The baby laughed and, for the first time ever, imitated Zayde perfectly. Our grandchild knew us both.

Our visit has been Grandparent Heaven. It has been filled with hugs, "besos for bebe" in honor of his Hispanic caregiver; beautiful smiles; hours reading *Go Dog Go* and *Brown Bear, Bear, Who Do You See?*; innumerable playings of songs by Rafi; multiple trips to city parks, a special day at the San Francisco zoo; and a few precious babysitting stints. As promised, I even pulled off two Shabbat dinners with fresh baked challahs and candle lighting via Zoom with the rest of our family.

Soon Larry and I will be heading for our second farklempt moment. We will be flying to Colorado to be united with Julie, Sam, and our Mountain Girl, again over fifteen months in the making. Yes, we have spent hours and hours on FaceTime with our Rocky Mountain family, but I will be overcome with emotion when I can finally hold them in our arms.

Throughout the past year, Larry and I have said again and again how grateful we are for our physical and financial health. But again and again, what we missed most was family. The next step will be getting all eight of us under one roof. That moment will be for me the end of this long, difficult time. Until then, I will savor our time with our family, time that has become even more precious, more important, and more cherished after being deprived for so long.

July 8, 2021

Chapter Thirty-Three

Farklempt: Part Two

U p until now, I thought that maybe I hadn't missed that much in the past 16 months. Larry and I had our health and had managed to keep a level of contentment throughout the pandemic. We missed our family terribly, but we had frequent Zoom calls with our children and grandchildren.

Even throughout our two weeks in California, I felt pretty good. Overwhelmed with emotion, Larry and I hugged our fifteen-and-a-half-month-old grandson. I knew I had missed a huge chunk of his first year, but I took comfort again from the hours on Zoom and FaceTime. We were starting our in-person relationship late, but I didn't dwell on what we had missed. He knew us. He came to us. We savored every minute of our visit with Adam, Sarah, and the beautiful little boy who had been named after two of his great grandfathers.

But then, after our flight to Denver and an easy drive on Interstate 70 to Summit County, we hugged our granddaughter. (She had been warned: We would be hugging her so hard that she would squeak!) But who was this taller, more beautiful, more poised person? Where was the little girl with whom we had last hugged goodbye in Florida in March 2020? The gap between her and this person who poured her own tea, rode a two-wheeler, and swam underwater in her community pool was so great. Yes, we had missed time with her, with her new cousin, with all my children that we can never make up.

And I hadn't realized how much I had missed our time in the mountains. On our third day, I finally made the hike up to Rainbow Lake, a short distance from our daughter's home and our summer rental. As I walked up the trail, I took in the columbines and the wild roses and the aspens. Then I reached the lake, my happy place, the spot in which I find peace and contentment. How could I have forgotten how much I love this spot over

9100 feet above sea level in the Rockies? Had it been almost two full years since I had sat on the log and drank in the beauty that surrounded me?

Larry and I had spent the Fourth of July in Frisco for at least ten years. We watched the parade march down Main Street with Sam and Julie, then, six years ago, Sam and a nine-month pregnant Julie. The next few years, our granddaughter watched from her carriage, then her father's arms, and then as a participant on a tricycle in the Cavalcade of Children.

This year, however, we headed out of town and by 11:30 a.m., five humans and one dog were floating down the Colorado River. Sam manned the raft while Julie completed the entire trip, including some level 1 and 2 rapids, on a paddle board. Larry, our granddaughter, and I found spots on the raft and took in the beauty surrounding us. We spotted a bald eagle perched in a tree, Canadian geese gliding along the shore, red cliffs rising above us, the Rocky Mountaineer weaving its way on the train tracks above us, fellow travelers on rafts and kayaks and paddle boards and inner tubes catching the currents with us. It was a beautiful Fourth, made even more special in contrast to last year's isolation in our Florida home.

The day ended with our granddaughter reading *Go Dog Go,* one of our favorite children's books, to Larry while sitting on his lap on a rocking chair in her bedroom. Behind them, the window gave us a view of the sun setting in the aspen trees.

As we finished our time in the mountains, Larry and I had also been able to connect with the friends and extended *mishpachah* that we had not seen since August 2019. We took in outdoor lunches and evening concerts with dear friends from North Carolina. We celebrated our granddaughter's birthday with Sam's family by riding the Georgetown Railroad, eating lunch alongside Clear Creek, and singing "Happy Birthday" over cupcakes and a candle-that-refused-to-stay-lit in a breezy park. After two full years, we are again finding our Colorado rhythm.

Mann Tracht, Un Gott Lacht is an old Yiddish expression meaning "man plans, and God laughs." Recent events have shown us how unpredictable life can be, whether exemplified in a terrible pandemic that has lasted for months or a catastrophic building collapse that happened in seconds. On a personal level, these past eight weeks of my reconnecting with family and friends have made me realize how much I missed, how much time I have lost, and how important it is to never take what I cherish for granted.

July 22, 2021

Chapter Thirty-Four

Pandemic In Three Pratfalls

On a beautiful morning in the Rockies, I wove my way up the two-mile Mont Royal Trail. Geared up in hiking boots, pants, and my new "Mountain Mama" T-shirt, I enjoyed the solitude, the sounds of mountain streams and chirping birds, and the sight of butterflies that lead me up the path. Small wooden bridges spanned the occasional creeks. Arriving on the bank of Rainbow Lake, I took in the beauty surrounding me before starting the trip down the Aspen Trail.

Despite my pure joy of being in my "happy place," I know my family worries about my frequent solo hikes. It would be generous to say their fear emanates from possible encounters with moose, elk, or bear. Unfortunately, it actually comes from encounters with rocks and roots. No, they don't fear my being eaten by a forest denizen. They fear I might trip on the gnarled tree roots, the patches of loose stone, or the small boulders that are a part of the hiking experience.

Not that their concerns are unfounded. Over the past 16 months, COVID-19 has not felled me. It has been my own stupid feet.

My first trip down free fall lane came early in the pandemic. With pools and exercise classes in our 55+ active community shuttered, Larry and I were taking one of our long morning walks. It was hot, as usual. It was humid, as usual. What wasn't usual was the dead snake lying on the sidewalk in front of us a mile into our walk.

"Watch out!" I yelled to Larry. He crossed his right leg in front of me to avoid the snake, and I fell fast. And hard. And as I slammed face first onto the pavement, all I could think was "Damn that snake!"

I felt incredible pain and tasted the blood that was pooling in front of me. For one of the few times in my life, I was grateful my nose was more

Barbra Streisand that Amy Adams, as it appeared to have taken most of the hit.

When I gingerly stood up, Larry and I assessed the damage. Scraped elbows and knees that did not require stitches? Check. Bones intact? Check. Teeth whole and still in mouth? Check. Ability to walk home? With the help of an ice pack wrapped in a towel provided by a Good Samaritan who had witnessed the accident from her front porch, also CHECK!

Fortunately, outside of two black eyes and multiple minor scrapes, I had avoided major injuries and a trip to the emergency room.

My second adventure in face plants occurred twelve months later when the world was finally opening up. Larry and I were visiting my brother and sister-in-law in Sarasota, Florida, the first time we had been able to connect with family since the coronavirus hit. On the second day of our visit, the four of us took a trip to Spanish Point, a 30-acre outdoor museum site. We were weaving through a section which was being set up for an evening concert. As I was wearing the required face mask, sunglasses, and a wide brimmed hat, I didn't see the sound bar the sound technician had placed between the bottom rungs of two chairs. My foot caught on the pole, and I did a hard splat in the grass. It was a second lucky "break" in that I walked away with a scraped-up face, another set of black eyes, and no ER visit.

Three months later, my luck ran out. Larry and I were in San Francisco visiting Adam, Sarah, and our sixteen-month-old grandson. On a Saturday morning, we took an easy, scenic three-mile round trip hike on the Tennessee Valley Trail in nearby Marin County. We were off the trail and walking to our parked car when I tripped over a stupid rock—or is it that stupid me tripped over an innocent rock? Fortunately, I fell right in front of a doctor and his family who were about to begin their hike. He bandaged me up with the diagnosis that nothing appeared to be broken, but the cut on my forearm was deep and required stitches.

After striking out at our attempts to get help at two urgent cares—one was closed; the second didn't do sutures—Adam dropped Larry and me off at the University of California San Francisco's emergency room. At first, judging from the number of people in the waiting area, I thought that I would get in and out quickly. Four and a half hours later, however, the ER manager announced that, along with those of us cooling our heels in the waiting room, there were at least 25 ambulances lined up outside with people in worse shape than us low priority patients with mere ear infections, head bumps, and cut forearms. We should expect a possible ten-hour wait.

I was about to ask for a sewing kit and a prescription for antibiotics and call it a day when—thank goodness—I was taken into a room to get patched up. Six stitches and a tetanus shot later, I was good to go. Thankfully, I have had no lingering effects from Pratfall #3.

Initially I was worried that maybe I was having balance issues. In the days and weeks that followed, others of all ages have told me of similar situations that resulted in much worse endings—broken elbows, wrists, and legs. Yes, I consider myself lucky.

As I was getting ready for my first solo hike in Colorado, Julie encouraged me to wait for her so that she could watch over me and make sure I didn't fall. I said no, insisting that this almost-71-year-old body was still more than capable of hiking up and down trails, thank you very much. She did meet me halfway and showed me a longer but less steep trail that I have taken on my own as well as others with Larry and my grand dog. Larry and I have also tackled longer, more difficult hikes without a scratch—or splat—between us.

Our most memorable Colorado hike this summer was the one Larry and I took with our granddaughter. When we reached the Rainbow Lake area, she insisted we ford a small stream by scrambling across the logs that spanned the water. Larry questioned whether she should attempt the crossing. "Don't worry, Zayde!" she said. "I'm a Mountain Girl! I got this." Taking my cue from her, I successfully made my way across the logs, albeit slower, more cautiously, and certainly more awkwardly. But I did it. After all, as my new T-shirt reflects, "I am a Mountain Mama. I got this!"

Epilogue: Soon after sharing this story with my writing group, Larry and I spent the afternoon exploring Vail Village. In Christy's Sports, I decided to try on a shirt that had caught my eye. As the salesperson led me to the changing rooms, he said, "Take the room on the left. There is a lip on the one on the right, and I won't want you to trip."

"Do I LOOK like someone who would trip?" I said.

He quickly backtracked. "Well, even sixteen-year-olds have tripped over it." Not surprisingly, I didn't buy the shirt. Before I left the store, however, I sought out the salesperson and gave him my business card with my blog address. "My next article will be The Pandemic in Three Pratfalls," I said. "Your comment will be in it!"

August 5, 2021

Chapter Thirty-Five

Fradel's Story: My Pandemic Project

W hat better way to start off a new year than to publish a new book? *Fradel's Story*, my third book since 2016, was especially sweet as it was co-written with my mother, Frances Cohen.

Ever since I could remember, my mother was the family storyteller. Give her an opening, and Fran, or "Fradel" as she was known to her close family, would regale any audience with stories of her grandparents'and parents' lives in Russia, her early years of marriage to "my Bill" Cohen, their life in small towns in the North Country. She told of raising four children, watching them leave for college and for marriage, and their returning with her grandchildren to visit her and my father in their beloved cottage on Lake Champlain.

As my parents got older, my mother realized that she needed to record these stories. We never were one for video camera and tapes, so she began jotting them down on lined paper, usually the five-by-eight notepads. The writing was messy, with misspellings and crosscuts, but she finally began to keep a written history.

In 2006, after a number of health setbacks, my three siblings, our spouses, and I insisted that my parents sell their condo in Florida and move back up north. That May, they moved into Coburg Village, an independent living facility only four miles from our home.

Soon after moving in, my mother called me to tell me she was joining Coburg's monthly writing group to finally finish all those stories she carried in her head and on those scraps of paper. When she brought her first story to the group, her accounting of why she and my father moved to the facility, she was surprised to find that the group enjoyed her writing style. "They loved my story, Marilyn!" she told me. "They said I have a real flair for storytelling!" After that, my mother's voice in phone calls after the monthly Wednesday meetings was filled with pride.

Mom rarely had difficulty finding a topic and writing it down with pen on paper. However, the group leader requested that the stories be typed so they could eventually be published in the semi-annual collection and distributed to Coburg residents. My mother asked me to type them. While I

109

was at it, could I, "My daughter the English major," do some proofing and minor revisions so that they would read more smoothly?

Thus began our five-year collaboration. Every month, about a week before the group met, my mother would give me her handwritten story. I would do some editing, including spelling, grammar, and even some tightening of the narrative. Her oral stories evolved into polished narratives, funny, poignant, sad, and sometimes painful, but always entertaining.

When my father passed away in November 2008, my mother's contribution for December was an open letter to my father. She wrote that she was moving into a smaller apartment down the hall. "Wherever I go, you also go in spirit," she wrote. Grieving quietly, she continued with her life at Coburg, going to the concerts, visiting with friends and family who were always stopping by to see her, and continuing with her writing. All the children asked her to write about our births and early childhood, but she always postponed those stories, focusing on the Old Country, her childhood, her Bill.

On December 22, 2010, my mother had a heart attack. The doctors recommended hospice care and living her remaining time to the fullest. She complied, enjoying visits and calls from the children, grandchildren, her extended family, and the many friends she and my father had made in Coburg and in their lifetimes. Despite her failing health, she kept writing.

In February 2011, with my sister Laura and me sitting close by, my mother shared her story, "The Birth of Laura, My First Child," with her writing group. She described her joy in having a beautiful little girl and her fears that she would not be able to be a good mother. The last words, written in pencil on the bottom, were "To be continued." She died four weeks later, the day of the club's March meeting.

I had made a promise to myself that one day I would gather her stories in a book. When COVID-19 shuttered so many of my activities, I decided that it was time. For eighteen pandemic months, I worked on editing, filling in the gaps, and finally arranging the stories in chronological order to make the book flow smoother.

I too had family stories, articles I had written over the years capturing memories of our old Victorian in Upstate New York, our cottage on Lake Champlain, my father's obsession with boats, bugs, and bats; my mother's words of wisdom; my siblings 'accomplishments. I decided to include those in the book.

By this March, I was ready to send my first draft to my editor, Mia Crews. She was responsible for formatting the book for paperback and Kindle as well as inserting the 80+ photos, many of them family pictures that dated back to 1914. *Fradel's Story* was launched on Amazon. It was in time for my target, September 1, 2021, what would have been my mother's 104th birthday.

My parents were not wealthy people. They had little of material value: a wedding ring, my Grandmother Ethel's engagement ring, two beautiful, framed pictures of my father at thirteen and my mother at six, a few nice dishes. As my siblings and I sadly dismantled Mom's apartment, my daughter was surprised that I wanted so little. "It's okay, Julie," I said. "I have her stories."

And now, I can share them with my large close-knit family, with an incredible network of friends who personally knew my parents or their legacy, and hopefully hundreds of others who may find their own lives reflected in this collection.

September 1, 2021

Chapter Thirty-Six

Hat Tricks

"I'm organized. I just can't find anything."
Saying on CJ Bella Co. Tea Towel

S pending a good part of this past summer in Colorado with our six-year-old granddaughter reaped incredibly wonderful moments for Larry and me. The first hugs after a year of seeing her only on Zoom. Reading her books and playing Candy Land and War and Pete's Birthday Party. Having her knock on the door of our rental at 8 a.m. on a Sunday morning with a newspaper in her hand and her announcement, "I am here for breakfast." I even extended my stay, so I was able to join Julie and Sam in walking my granddaughter to her first day of first grade. I made enough memories to almost sustain me until we can see her again.

What was not incredibly wonderful was keeping track of all the items our six-year-old dynamo left behind. Larry and I had rescued her baseball butterfly hat from the Frisco Recreation Center's lost and found. Julie found her lost raincoat at her Fun Club two weeks after my granddaughter had left it there. In the meantime, Julie had to buy another one in a larger size. It was a little big, but Summit County was getting above average rain in July, and there was no choice.

Both Julie and Sam dealt with the lost-and-found problem quite calmly—to a point. But when Julie realized that their daughter's favorite hat was missing the day before they were to leave for their planned one-week rafting trip, well, Julie lost it—her cool that is!

The first we heard about the missing hat was on the Sunday morning before their trip.

"Come over for pancakes," Julie's text read. "And can you check your condo to see if you have the butterfly hat?"

Yes, Mountain Girl was wearing a hat on Friday. She had it in the car when we drove down to Main Street for some bubble tea at the Next Page Book Store. In the picture I had taken of her sitting on Zayde's lap listening to a story in the town promenade, she was hatless. But I vaguely remember taking the floppy hat festooned with butterflies and dragon flies from her outstretched hand before she hung upside down from the ropes at the playground in Walter Byron Park. I thought I had stuffed it in my pocket and returned it safely when we drove her home.

But Julie reported it wasn't in their house. And it did not appear to be in our condo. Or in our car. Or at the condo's pool area. When we arrived at their house that morning, Julie was flipping her oatmeal pancakes with obvious annoyance.

"I can't believe that people don't keep track of her things when they are responsible for watching her," she said, digging her barbs into both her parents and poor Sam. "First one hat; then a raincoat, now another hat! Doesn't anyone ever check to see if she has left anything behind?"

Even though I was thinking, "Maybe the *child* needs to be responsible!" I kept my mouth closed. Besides, Julie's guilt trip was working. After breakfast, I walked the two minutes back to our rental and did a second, more thorough search. I checked pockets and backpacks and drawers. I checked under the bed and under the couch and under the seats of our car. It was nowhere to be found.

By the time I got back to their house, Julie and Sam were fully engaged in getting ready for their seven-day trip. Having to limit myself to under fifty pounds of stuff for our nine weeks out west, it admittedly looked easier than gathering everything they needed for camping and rafting. Larry and I entertained our granddaughter with books, puzzles, and games, trying to stay out of the way of the oars, coolers, rucksacks stuffed with clothing and towels, bottles of suntan lotion and bug spray, sleeping bags, a paddle board, and enough food and drink for a small army.

By the time we finished lunch, I needed a break and a possible chance at redemption.

"I'm walking downtown to see if I can find the lost hat," I said. "If that fails, I will see if I can find a replacement."

I first checked the bookstore's lost and found. Lots of sunglasses and a set of keys, but no hat. I then walked through Walter Byron Park. Someone had hung up a slightly worn "Get high in Colorado" T-shirt on the park sign, but no hat. I then walked back to Main Street and began checking out the hat racks that were set up in front of many of the stores, another exercise in futility. Too big. Too small. Wrong print. Wrong color. I stuck on my mask and began checking out inside inventories. I finally saw a possibility. Right size. Pink (Her favorite color). No butterflies, but lots of bright flowers. I snapped a picture and texted it to Julie. Getting no response, I followed it up with a phone call.

"The hat wasn't in the bookstore or the park, so I decided to check the stores," I said. "Look at the picture on your text. I think you will love it."

"Mom," Julie replied a few seconds later. "The hat is adorable, but we are not missing the floppy dragonfly hat. We are missing the baseball butterfly cap!"

"She wasn't wearing her *baseball* butterfly cap on Friday," I said testily. "She was wearing her *floppy* butterfly hat."

"That's her dragonfly hat as it has dragonflies *and* butterflies," Julie said. "We have that one!" Then she added sheepishly, "I guess you and Dad didn't lose it after all." Long pause. "Hey, at least you got your exercise in!"

She was right. By the time I got home, I had walked over three miles looking for a hat that we had never lost in the first place.

I also realized that we had seen a girl's butterfly baseball cap the day before at the REI in the next town over. I called the outdoor retailer and asked the clerk to put it aside for my daughter. No longer feeling magnanimous or generous, I made no move to pick up either the hat or the cost. After realizing the Fun Club lost and found box was locked up because of a field trip, Julie drove to Silverthorne and bought it herself.

The following Sunday night, Julie, Sam, and my granddaughter returned from their camping trip. First thing on Monday morning, Mother and Daughter walked over to Fun Club, where the missing hat was waiting in the lost and found box.

"This warrants a story, you realize," I told her the next day while sitting at her kitchen table with my computer. Julie just shrugged. And I started typing away.

September 16, 2021

Chapter Thirty-Seven

Bye Bye Boomer

W as it time for us to retire Boomer to that Stuffed Bear Den in the Sky?

A couple of days after Adam was born, Larry came to St Peter's hospital with a huge brown teddy bear, his first gift to Adam. We named the stuffy "Boomer," the moniker we had given to my ever-expanding stomach during my pregnancy as well as a salute to our Baby Boomer status.

Boomer occupied a place in Adam's room in our family home through nursery school and beyond. When the shiny nose fell off, I sewed on another one with black yarn. When the paws got torn up after too many rides on Adam's Big Wheels, I covered up the bear's bare spots with yellow felt patches. Even when Adam left for college and Boomer was bursting at the seams, I patiently sewed up his side and his legs.

In the end, Larry and I loved Boomer more than Adam did. By his bar mitzvah, Adam had relegated Boomer to the top shelf in his bedroom. When Adam headed off to the University of Rochester in 1996, he left him behind. We put the brown bear on the pillow on Adam's bed in the quiet, empty, amazingly clean room. Boomer waited patiently through Adam's grad school and first jobs and trips across country and to Israel and Belize and law school. Alas, Adam never sent for him.

Three years after Adam's departure, Julie brought her own lovey, a bear named Rerun, with her to college. It now has a place of honor on her daughter's bed.

When we packed up to move to Florida, I sent texts to our children with pictures of the things they left behind with the simple request: "Toss or send to you?" Adam claimed his Star Wars action figures, Zayde Ernie's World War II helmet, and a couple of framed pictures. Boomer got a thumbs down.

Larry and I didn't have the heart to throw Boomer in the trash. After some discussion, we carted him to Kissimmee, where he earned a spot on a bookshelf with our other cherished *tchotchkes*: Larry's Otto the Orange mascot, a plush toy I had given him one Hanukkah that played the Syracuse University's marching song when we squeezed his hand. My two 7-inch-high dolls in Mexican attire my father had purchased for me at a gift shop in Montreal's Chinatown after wontons and fortune cookies at the Nan King restaurant. Julie's doll with the green dress and matching bonnet that had prompted our then-fourteen-month-old daughter's first complete sentence on the way back from a shopping trip to buy her a bed: "Oh-oh! Left Baby Bobbie on mattress at Macy's," she cried behind me from her car seat. "Go back!"

I thought Boomer would find his way back home to Adam when Sarah delivered their own little Boomer in 2020. My hopes that I could pack him up in a box and ship him to California were quickly dashed. "I certainly don't want it," Adam told me. "And after 42 years, goodness knows what germs live in that toy. Toss it."

Taking a good look at Boomer, I almost had to agree with Adam. I took pride in the fact that the black nose and yellow felt paws and feet I had sewn on over forty years ago were still intact. After too many years dealing with Florida humidity, however, the poor stuffed animal was definitely worse for wear. His now graying stuffing was peeking out of his right leg and exploding out of a side seam. His head wobbled, held onto the body with unraveling brown thread. His "fur" had begun to resemble that of a mangy dog. Still, we put him back on the shelf.

Eighteen months later, Boomer's future was again in jeopardy. Larry and I had managed to fit all that was needed for a seven-week trip to visit our children in California and Colorado in two medium-sized suitcases. If we had survived all summer with so little, why were our closets and drawers still packed with all the clothes we hadn't bothered to bring?

It wasn't just the clothes. Despite our purge when we made the move to Florida from Upstate New York in 2015, we (especially me) had somehow again acquired too much stuff. A kitchen full of housewares. Closets filled with unworn clothing. Old books that I planned to read while sheltering in place. A two-foot stack of nearly untouched *New Yorker* magazines. I was ready for a pandemic purge. The day before Rosh Hashanah, while looking in my closet to find an outfit for services, I found two dresses that I had not worn in three years. I threw them onto the guest bed. I followed them up with more items to recycle—clothes, linens, books, heavy sweaters I had saved "just in case." By Yom Kippur, the pile covered the entire double bed. It was a new year, a new start.

But some things were non-recyclable, including a tattered teddy. "Maybe it's time to say goodbye to Boomer," I said to Larry.

"No way!" he cried. "Besides, we need to keep him at least until our grandson is able to come to Florida to visit. He has to meet Boomer."

Larry was right. The idea of putting Boomer into the trash broke both our hearts. I took out my sewing kit, pushed the stuffing back into worn cloth, and stitched him up, using patches as needed. I bought a Size 2T toddler shirt covered with bears and moose and pulled it over Boomer's head to cover up all the stitches. And then Boomer resumed his special place on our shelf. Yes, in the end, we couldn't—forgive the pun—*bear* to part with him.

October 1, 2021

Chapter Thirty-Eight

Mountain Mama

Don't ask what the world needs. Ask what makes you come alive and go do it. Because what the world needs is people who have come alive.
Howard Thurman

O n one of our FaceTime calls early in the pandemic, my daughter Julie was sporting a grey sweatshirt with a bright psychedelic mountain design and the words *Mountain Mama* emblazoned on it. "I love your sweatshirt," I said. "Where did you get it?"

Julie shared with me that she had purchased it on-line from Sunny Side Up, a local business in her Summit County, Colorado, community. Following Julie's directions, I purchased one and had it shipped to our Florida home. I loved wearing my new top with leggings or yoga pants during Florida's "winter," the months that even Florida gets cold enough for warm clothes.

More importantly, I loved the idea that I was supporting a local business. The path of destruction created by the pandemic is well-known: disrupted lives, cancelled events, shuttered businesses, parents scrambling to help their children with on-line learning, short and long-term illness, and, of course, over 700,000 deaths in the United States alone. But one of the positives I have seen again and again is what is known in Judaism as *akehillah kadoshah,* a holy community when people demonstrate caring and compassion that comes with the feeling that its members matter to each other. One place this expression of taking care of each other was in the story of Ash Weisel's unique gift shop in a small town located two hours west of Denver at 9100 feet in the Rocky Mountains.

Ashlie Barclay Weisel was born and raised in Crown Point, Indiana, a small town 50 miles southeast of Chicago. She and husband Dan Weisel were high school sweethearts and were married in 2009. After graduation, Dan enlisted in the Air Force, and they spent the first four years in Germany. While there, Ash was smitten by the mountains, the small, picturesque towns, and the beautiful architecture. Ash also loved the opportunity and freedom their time overseas offered to her. "I could pull out my sketch book and create free-flowing fun designs wherever I was," said Ash, "whether it be beside a German stream or on an airplane."

When they returned to the States, Dan enrolled in the University of Colorado, Boulder, and Ash continued free-lance illustration and setting up her happy art around art festivals in Colorado. She loved and followed the brand, Be Hippy, and started designing for them after meeting them at a festival in Keystone.

Two years later, with her confidence boosted by the popularity of her designs with Be Hippy, Ash decided to venture out on her own. On their anniversary trip, Ash and Dan stopped in Frisco, Colorado, and Ash immediately was reminded of towns they had visited in Germany. Although they lived in Colorado's Front Range at the time, Ash split her time between Summit County and their home near Denver. Soon after, Dan, who was employed as a state patrol officer, had a job transfer to Frisco, and Ash began working for the art district in Breckenridge .

When space for a store opened in 2018, they jumped at the chance to open her own business. She had found a home for her art and her positive outlook on life at her new store, Sunny Side Up, where she could "sell happiness."

"At our home in Germany, my personal art studio was on the second floor with a sunny terrace attached," Ash said. "I named the store Sunny Side Up in honor of our four years in that wonderful country."

A bright, breezy shop with a definite 1970s hippy vibe, the store displayed Ash's own original artwork and offered tables for people to relax and create their own art projects supplemented by Sunny Side Up's supplies and inspiration. By summer of 2019 the business had been successful enough for her to open a second location in nearby Breckinridge.

Then, in March 2020, COVID-19 struck. Governor Jared Polis announced that all non-essential businesses were to close. Ash was forced to give up the Breckinridge store. Meanwhile, how could she and Dan continue to operate a business with no customers?

Initially, Ash established an "honesty shop," where she set up her T-shirts, mugs, and affirmation posters in front of the store with envelopes available so people could slip the money for the purchases under the door.

Just before the pandemic, Ash had designed a sweatshirt that she felt captured the Rocky Mountain spirit. The front of the slate grey hoodie was emblazoned with a colorful hippy-feel mountain design with the words "Mountain Mama" written across the top. With hundreds sitting unsold because of the shutdown, she decided to cut the price and sell them online to keep her store afloat. Cayla, her co-worker, along with friends, hand delivered the orders to local customers. Through word of mouth and Mountain Mama sightings, sales grew as more and more women, stuck at home, donned Ash's creation over their sweatpants. Before she knew it, Ash had sold 200 of her tops.

Women began posting pictures on social media as a statement of solidarity in tough times. "Everyone just flocked to them," said Weisel. "The sweatshirt really became a symbol of hope and unity in our little mountain town."

Shannon Noel Bosgraaf, a local realtor and Ash's friend, photoshopped dozens of the individual pictures into one huge poster with the logo 'Mountain Mamas: Stronger Together!'

"The community of women became super excited to show off their support, and it gave us all a focus on something bigger than ourselves," said Shannon.

In April 2020, Denver's 9News picked up the story, and sales went through the roof. "A lot of people are calling it their quarantine uniform," Ash said in the televised interview. "The demand is so high we have had people all over the nation say they want them."

To date, Weisel has sold over 2000 Mountain Mama and, for those without children, Mountain Chick sweatshirts. Ash replicated the design on T-shirts and hats, which were sold in the store once the pandemic shutdown ended. When I visited the store this past summer, the place was buzzing with people purchasing Ash's designs, including several variations of the Mountain Mama theme.

Ash is now moving Sunny Side Up in a new direction. She is closing the working studio section of her store and using the space to sell more of her own creations in clothing and accessories. She has renamed her store to Stay Sunny Goods. Meanwhile, the original Mountain Mama trademark logo is being retired.

Will she create a new one?

"I have thought about it," Weisel said. "But I haven't been inspired to come up with a new design yet."

I have confidence that Ash, a self-proclaimed 'purveyor of positives, ' will follow her muse and design more Mountain Mama products. Shannon Bosgraaf, the friend who put together the collage said, "When I see someone today with the sweatshirt, it reminds me of that pure joy that we, together as a community, created and Ash's amazing inspiration and art was able to continue."

October 4, 2021

Chapter Thirty-nine

Weathering The Storm

"When you come out of the storm, you won't be the same person who walked in. That's what this storm's all about."
Haruki Murakami

Ever since the first cases of COVID-19 were identified, America has been divided regarding wearing masks, gathering in large groups, or, most recently, getting one of the variants of the vaccine. Heated arguments have occurred in government institutions to sports venues to houses of worship to classrooms to local bridge groups. For Kathy Glascott, a COVID-19 survivor, such protocols are not a matter of personal choice but a matter of social responsibility.

A former elementary school teacher from Buffalo, New York, Kathy Glascott was the happiest she had been in many years. She had retired to Solivita, a 55-plus community near Orlando, Florida. As was her style, she showed up for life. She was involved in several activities including the British Isles Heritage Club, the Western Upstate New York club, and SOL Writers. A widow, she met her significant other, Mike, through the community's singles group, and they were having fun, going to concerts and dances and traveling to places of which she had only dreamed. "It was like being a teenager again," she said.

Then, in February 2020, the unsettling news of a virus later identified as COVID-19 began to emerge. Heeding the early advice of medical experts, Kathy sheltered in place and tried to avoid exposure. One day, short on groceries, she took a risk and went for a quick supermarket run. "I didn't have a mask because you couldn't get them," Kathy reflected months later. "Looking back, I wish I'd had the damn groceries delivered."

Soon after, Kathy began to feel unwell. One evening, exhausted and exhibiting symptoms of what she thought was bronchitis exacerbated by her asthma, she had Mike take her to the nearby hospital's ER. She had no idea that it would be 5 1/2 months until she would see anyone except through a plate glass door.

Kathy was diagnosed with bilateral pneumonia and COVID-19. She was almost immediately placed in an induced coma in the ICU. She had only vague memories of anything from March 27 until she woke up on May 5. "During that time," she wrote months later, "my body was assaulted by machines that were surrogates for bodily organs—a feeding tube, a respirator, and catheters."

Meanwhile, her brother Brian Joyce, a Methodist pastor in New Jersey, kept her large family and many friends abreast of Kathy's life and death struggle through posts on her popular Facebook page. On three occasions, Brian gave the grim news that she had been intubated and was near death. Even when the medical staff removed her from her induced coma, she was not out of the woods. She remained hospitalized for another six weeks and later continued her recovery in a rehab center where she had to learn again to hold her head up, sit, stand, walk, and swallow.

Brian warned his Facebook followers against what he called "COVID-19 fairytales." "It would be nice if Kathy's story demonstrated a victory over the virus," he posted on August 1, 2020, as his sister entered her 19th week of fighting for her life. "In reality her recovery is a daily journey through pain, loneliness, separation, therapy, small victories, and moments of great success and rising hope."

On September 6, 163 days after she had been admitted to the hospital, Kathy was finally released. For the first two months, she stayed with her neighbor and closest friend Susan Schulman. After Kathy moved back into her own home, she continued to rely on Susan, Mike, and others to provide a much-needed network of support.

Over eighteen months later, Kathy is still trying to make sense of what happened and to fix what's broken. She mourns the six months of her life she lost to the virus in which her only contacts were her ever-present, albeit wonderful medical staff members.

Although not confirmed by her doctors, Kathy considers herself as a "long hauler," one of unfortunate 10% of COVID-19 survivors who experiences prolonged effects of the illness. In her case, she struggles with vision problems, a chronic cough, reoccurring bronchitis, neuropathy in her feet, frequent fatigue, and bouts of PTSD. "I'm better, but I'm not the me I was before COVID-19," wrote Kathy on a post in her blog *This and That:*

Musings on Being a Writer. "I have a new normal that makes me fee. diminished, stressed, joyful, discouraged, and grateful all at the same time.'

Kathy also recognizes that COVID-19 has affected not only herself bu also those with whom she is involved. This is especially seen in the impac her illness had on her daughter, Brenda Glascott, a college administrato who lives with her wife in Portland, Oregon. "Ever since I woke her in the middle of the night on March 28 to say, 'I love you 'before I was intubatec for the first time, Brenda has had to make a number of hard decisions on my behalf," said Kathy. "And she made each one with courage and love." Kathy said that the hope of seeing her daughter and others she loved sustained her and kept her fighting in her darkest hours.

Kathy was and continues to be an outspoken opponent of those whc reject measures regarding mask wearing, vaccines, and social distancing or the pretext of personal freedom. "If you hate wearing a mask," read one o her 2021 Facebook posts, "you're really not going to like the ventilator." In another post, she quoted George Takei, the American actor and activist. "Telling me that you are proudly unvaccinated is like telling me that you're a drunk driver. You're not a patriot. You're not a freedom fighter. You're a menace."

As a survivor, Kathy feels a responsibility to protect herself and others even now. "I try to honor the concern and love shown to me by not taking unnecessary chances and by practicing safe protocols." Those measures include limiting her exposure to others and wearing a mask in crowds even though she is fully vaccinated.

A writer and author of three previous books, Kathy is working on a fourth that will recount in detail her own harrowing dance with COVID-19. "When I think about the many people who were affected by my struggle, I am humbled by their love and concern and grateful for the outpouring o prayer and support I received," she said. "I hope to pay it forward by sharing my own experience and encouraging others to take the necessary steps to protect themselves and help curtail the spread and continuance of this terrible pandemic."

October 28, 2021

Chapter Forty

Close Encounters Of The Moose Kind

Blessed art thou, O Lord our G-d, King of the Universe, who created beautiful animals in His world.
(Berahot 9)

I have much for which to be thankful this Thanksgiving. We have just returned from a trip to visit our children and their families. Our family has survived a pandemic with the help of the COVID-19 vaccine for everyone six and over. Most recently, I am thankful that our close encounters of the wild kind have ended well for both us and the animals.

As Upstate New Yorkers, Larry and I rarely encountered threatening animals. Yes, we watched out for rattlesnakes while hiking the eponymous trail in Lake George. And, yes, our cat's frequent encounters with skunks showed us the unpleasant scent of nature. But the closest I had come for most of my life to seeing animals-gone-wild was when we woke up to the sight of a herd of cows that had somehow escaped from a nearby farm grazing on the lawn of my parents' cottage on Lake Champlain. When we opened the door to take a closer look, our Irish setter ran out and started barking at them, triggering a mini stampede. At that exact moment, our neighbor Yolanda opened up her drapes to see a bunch of berserk bovines charging toward her sliding glass door. Local lore is that her screams still can be heard echoing throughout Willsboro Bay.

My first encounter with more dangerous beasts came in a 2012 trip to Florida.

While Larry and I were waiting for the guided tour tram to take us through the Shark River section of the Everglades, I spotted a huge alligator less than 10 feet away. Naive—make that stupid!—me insisted Larry take my picture while I was kneeling near its tail. When I proudly showed the picture to one of the guides a short time later, she warned me against a repeat performance. "Alligators may look slow, but they can move quickly," she said. "You were lucky you weren't bitten."

After that encounter combined with research and "alligators in the news" stories, I now have a much deeper appreciation of these ancient reptiles. We usually have at least one alligator in the pond in our backyard, either sunning itself on the bank or floating just below the surface. It is not unusual to see one crossing the road or even lounging in a doorway of an open garage in our community. Just this morning, a neighbor posted on our Next-Door website, "Please be careful. There is a large gator crossing the road on its way to Glendora Lakes." We have learned to live side by side with them by maintaining a healthy distance when walking near water and encouraging our guests to do the same.

Ever since her move to Colorado in 2003, Julie has shared with us her frequent close encounters with Rocky Mountain wildlife. On a run during her first month there, she had to detour to avoid a brown bear who was helping itself to an unlatched garbage bin. Stories of other unexpected meetups with more bears, as well as elk, moose, fox, and coyotes, have always been part of our conversations with Julie and Sam.

Julie and Sam are both experienced backpackers and outdoors people, sharing that knowledge with their Mountain Girl. When they are hiking, they can recognize the presence of animals by their hoof prints as well as their scat (poop). They also know what to do when they encounter an animal, whether it be on the trail or in their backyard. Like alligators, the best approach is to distance oneself from any wild animal to avoid a confrontation.

Despite all their experiences, Larry and I had only seen wildlife from a safe distance. That changed this summer. We hiked up a popular trail and made our usual left turn only to find a huge moose less than fifteen feet away. We quickly and quietly turned around and headed down the same trail.

I shared the news with several friends on social media, many whose first question was, "Did you get a picture?"

"No," I responded. "We just got the hell out of there!"

After waiting 18 years for our "Close Encounter of the Wild Kind," I was not expecting to see another moose until 2039. However, less than three months later, on an early November before-the-snow-falls trip, my grand dog Neva and I took a hike up to Rainbow Lake, my favorite spot in the world. On the way down, with only a slight pull on Neva's leash as a warning, I caught sight of the back end of a moose in the trees about 10 yards in front of us. Now the seasoned moose-avoider, I quickly got us "the hell out of there."

While winding our way down a longer but hopefully safer trail, Neva pulled hard on the leash, straining to run after something. *Oh no!* I thought, *Not another moose!* No, it was just a squirrel, which our grand dog obviously rated higher on the "wildlife-to-chase" scale than an unpredictable half-ton mammal. So much for feeling safer when hiking with my grand dog.

Moose sightings continued. Later that day, Larry and I avoided stepping in the piles of moose scat that adorned lawns and sidewalks in the neighborhood. We learned later that soon after trick or treaters had headed home with their junk food stash, the moose had moved in and devoured all the Halloween pumpkins.

The next morning, we were woken up to the sounds of our granddaughter clambering down the steps to the guest bedroom, yelling, "Moose alert! Moose alert! A mommy and her two calves are in our front yard!"

Larry and I are now back in Florida, but we need to remain on the lookout. Oh, well. At least alligators don't leave scat.

November 18, 2021

Chapter Forty-One

Mister Rogers

The murder of eleven Jews while they were attending Shabbat services occurred in the heart of Mister Rogers' Neighborhood.

The Reverend Fred Rogers and his wife Joanne owned a home and raised their two sons in Squirrel Hill, just two blocks from Tree of Life, the scene of the October 27, 2018, massacre.

Who was Fred Rogers? Why did his former neighbors in this predominantly Jewish section of Pittsburgh turn to Mister Rogers for comfort after the tragedy? And why, seventeen years after his death, has he become *everyone's* favorite neighbor?

For several months, I had been reading reviews and seeing the trailers for *A Beautiful Day in the Neighborhood*, the biopic starring Tom Hanks. I decided I wanted to learn more about Rogers before I headed to the multiplex. I borrowed from our library Maxwell King's biography *The Good Neighbor: The Life and Works of Fred Rogers*. I found the well-written, thorough account compelling and—well—fascinating.

I was surprised. To be honest, I had not been a huge fan of the pleasant, bland man in the zippered knitted sweater and blue sneakers. My children frequently watched him when the show aired on our local public broadcasting station (PBS). For me, the timing was perfect, as it acted as a calm, caring babysitter as I prepared dinner. Years later, my children had only vague memories of watching the program.

But there was much to learn about the man behind the myth. I read about his difficult, lonely childhood in Latrobe, Pennsylvania; the taunts and bullying he endured ("Here comes Fat Freddy!"), and the respect he earned from his high school classmates through his music and leadership roles. I read about his meeting his wife Joanne at Rollins College, whose beautiful campus in Winter Park, less than an hour from us, has been a favorite place for us to visit.

Rogers originally planned on a career as a musician. After viewing television's early programming, ("There were people throwing *pies* at one another!") he decided that he wanted to find some "way of using this fabulous instrument to be of nurture to those who would watch and listen." And who best to nurture than preschoolers?

His initial television experiences were in New York and Toronto, first behind the scenes as a puppeteer and later reluctantly as a person in front of the camera. His interest in public television and the promise of commercial-free programming led to his move to Pittsburgh to join the local National Educational Television (changed to Public Broadcasting Corporation [PBS] in 1970) WQED in 1953.

Rogers went back to college in his thirties to complete a divinity degree and was an ordained Presbyterian minister. His lifelong interest in religion and theology expanded to his studying Catholic mysticism, Judaism, Buddhism, and other faiths. Most importantly, Rogers' values were those shared by all religions: civility, tolerance, sharing, and self-worth. Combined with his grandfather's affirmation to his sickly, over-protected grandchild, "I like you just the way you are," these principals shaped not only the person but also the message he repeatedly emphasized in all 912 episodes of *Mister Rogers' Neighborhood.*

Despite his saintly, other-worldly demeanor, Rogers—as his wife repeatedly proclaimed—was NOT a saint. He had a temper and was prone to self-doubt and depression. In order to vent after a bad day, he would bang loudly on the piano. In one of my favorite passages in King's book, Rogers stubbornly refused to give into the demands of PBS executives regarding a small element of the script, and angry words flew. "Tell me," one of the executives said to the other, "how old do you have to be before Mister Rogers no longer likes you just the way you are?"

Armed with all this knowledge, I recently went to see *A Beautiful Day in the Neighborhood.* I was surprised that the script, based on a 1999 Esquire article by Tom Junod, focused less on Tom Hanks' Fred Rogers character and more on the troubled angry reporter who is assigned to interview the television icon. But I loved the story, the acting, and the cinematography, which included miniature scenery that captured the colors and scale of the original set.

In one of the tenderest moments in the movie, which was based on a real-life incident, Fred Rogers was riding on a New York City subway filled mostly with Black and Hispanic children on their way home from school. Rather than approaching him for an autograph, the children quietly began singing "Won't You Be My Neighbor?" the program's theme song. Soon, the entire car joined in. It brought tears to Mister Rogers' eyes—and mine.

As noted in both the book and the movie, Rogers had never been afraid to tackle difficult topics for preschoolers—the death of a pet, sibling rivalry, divorce, and the assassination of Robert Kennedy. Whether through his well-worn puppets in the Neighborhood of Make-Believe or through his field trips, Mister Rogers reassured children that there was good in the world.

The last episode of *Mister Rogers' Neighborhood* was recorded on December 1, 2000 and aired on August 31, 2001. Rogers then came out of retirement to tape shows focused on the September 11 terrorist attacks. He initially expressed concern that the specials would be of little value but then turned to a basic Jewish tenant to support his decision to go forward. "We all are called to be *tikkun olam*, repairers of creation," he said.

On September 11, 2002, he shared his first anniversary message on prime time. "I'm just so proud of all of you," Rogers told his viewers. "And I know how tough it is some days to look with hope and confidence on the months and years ahead." Soon after, Fred Rogers was diagnosed with advanced stomach cancer and passed away in February 2003.

Mister Robers' Neighborhood continued on PBS as reruns. In 2006, Fred Rogers Productions began the development of Daniel Tiger's Neighborhood, an animated children's television series based on Rogers ' Neighborhood of Make Believe and premiered the show on PBS Kids on September 3, 2012.

On December 12, 2012, a 20-year-old killed 26 people, including 20 children, at Sandy Hook Elementary School in Newtown, Connecticut. In the midst of parents trying to explain the inexplicable to their own children, the organization of 170 Million Americans for Public Broadcasting shared on the internet an image of a tiny boy cradling Mister Rogers' face. It was accompanied by a passage from his 1983 book, *Mister Rogers Talks to Parents*: "When I was a boy and I would see scary things in the news, my mother would say to me, 'Look for the helpers. You will always find people who are helping.' To this day, especially in times of disaster, I remember my mother's words." The image went viral on Facebook. Within three days, it was shared over 88,000 times.

The helper quote went viral again after the 2013 Boston Marathon bombing, the 2017 Manchester Arena bombing, and the 2018 Marjory Stoneman Douglas High School shooting in Parkland, Florida. As Aisha Harris wrote in a 2013 article for *Slate*, "[The message] serves not only as a comfort to kids, but to adults as well, a reminder to ourselves that there is still much good amid the bad."

The message was especially poignant for his former neighbors after an anti-Semite gunned down Jewish worshippers in Pittsburg on October 17, 2018. The Fred Rogers Center, established at St. Vincent's College, Latrobe, Pennsylvania under Rogers 'guidance before his death, immediately posted on their Facebook page a message tying the tragedy to Squirrel Hill's favorite neighbor. "We're holding Squirrel Hill in our thoughts today. While we always believe in 'looking for the helpers, 'we long for a day when there is no more tragedy born from hatred."

In an article published soon after in *Yahoo* news, Karen Struble Meyers, spokesperson for the Center, reflected on the question as to what

Mister Rogers would say. "Despite the deep grief in neighborhoods across the country, he would encourage us, just as he did after 9/11, to be good neighbors and to help the children in our lives to feel safe. His affirming message about our inherent likability and worth would bring comfort to many."

Mister Rogers' legacy lives on not only through his quotes but also through television, books, movies, DVD's, the Internet, and most recently in art. In October 2021, Rollins College unveiled a life-sized statue by British artist Paul Grey depicting the spirit of its most beloved graduate. The front of the sculpture reveals Mister Rogers in his signature sweater and sneakers, holding Daniel Striped Tiger and surrounded by children. When Larry and I finally left our COVID-19 cocoon to visit the Winter Park campus to view the statue, I reflected upon my granddaughter's love for the sometimes timid and sometimes brave striped tiger. As a preschooler, she spent hours watching *Daniel* videos and playing with miniatures of the Tiger family. "Daniel Tiger is always doing something new," she announced after we had read together on FaceTime her copy of the book *A Busy Day in the Neighborhood.* "I just like him." And then she sang. "It's a beautiful day in the neighborhood, a beautiful day." I happily joined in, wiping tears from my eyes.

Originally published December 26, 2019; Updated for this book.

Chapter Forty-Two

I Am Exactly Where I Need To Be

Have you kept your New Year's resolution?

Odds are, you haven't. Each year, Strava, the social network for athletes, predicts the exact day when most people are likely to ditch their annual commitment to themselves. Whether it be the goal to lose weight, exercise more, or stop smoking, the majority throw in the towel (or throw out the scale) on the second Friday in January. A full 80% will have given up on it by mid-February.

If you have made it past the day this issue of *The Jewish World* was published, *Mazel tov!*

Up until this year, my list of resolutions was endless, so reflective of the person I am. On top of my list (for at least six decades) was to lose weight. Along with that annual goal, I have promised myself in the past to exercise more, read more books, watch more movies, play more piano, see more of family and friends, and write more articles, for starters.

But as I head into a third year where pandemic still hangs over our heads like the sword of Damocles, I have made peace with myself. My one and only resolution is based on an affirmation I stumbled across this fall. Drum roll please!

"I am exactly where I need to be."

These eight words summarize an entire philosophy based on the idea that I can be happy where I am at this exact moment. It has grounded me when I find my mind racing with what I need to do next: the challah that needs to be baked; the article I have to get to Laurie Clevenson at *The Jewish World* by the Monday morning deadline; the library book I have to finish before it disappears off my Kindle.

Full disclosure: Knowing myself, I will still be working on those same items I have listed in the past. (I am already looking forward to writing several biographies of Holocaust survivors.) But I understand that I can reach those milestones without the help and pressure of resolutions. I can be happy in the "now," not the future. I have given myself permission to focus on the journey, not some numerical destination.

Since I made this resolution on November 17, I already have over two months of practice behind me. I made a copy of it which I keep on my kitchen counter. When I find myself "falling off the wagon," I quietly recite it to myself and get grounded again. It has the making of a habit! And speaking of habits…

I cannot remember where I originally saw this quote. Facebook? A friend's blog? A recent book? It took me a few weeks—and the help from my Catholic friend—to find that my first-person quote originally came from a prayer from St. Teresa of Avila, a revered leader of the Discalced Carmelite Sisters in sixteenth-century Spain. The opening lines of her original prayer read, "May today there be peace within you. Trust God that you are exactly where you are meant to be."

It took a little more digging to find a Jewish connection. Yes! There **IS** a Jewish connection! St. Teresa's paternal grandfather, a wealthy tax collector, was a Jew who was forced to convert to Christianity during the Spanish Inquisition. He was condemned for allegedly returning to the Jewish faith and was punished by being forced to parade around Toledo for one day a week with other insincere converts. He was later able to assume a Catholic identity.

St. Teresa, aware of her ancestry, did not acknowledge it publicly because of prejudice at the time against Jews and Jewish converts. It appeared, however, that her heritage impacted her career in the church. She was recognized for bring a mystical Jewish strain reminiscent of *Kabbalah* and for giving comfort to many converts from Judaism who struggled to maintain a connection to Jewish belief and practice. As a leader and "doctor," she directed her convents not to comply with the "statutes of purity of blood" which excluded Jewish converts to Catholicism from most religious orders, from the military, higher education, civil and church offices.

In the 2012 off-Broadway play, *Teresa's Ecstasy*, starring its Columbian playwright Begonya Plaza, Linda Larkin, and Shawn Elliott, the nun's Jewish heritage was seen as a driving force in her life and work. Plaza's character, who in the midst of a divorce, and Larkin's character, her Jewish lesbian lover, realize how much Teresa has become their role model in her commitment to faith, compassion, and human dignity. Yes, St. Teresa is a nun with a *Yiddishkeit neshome*, a Jewish soul.

So now an adaption of a prayer written by a Catholic saint is now part of my daily routine. It is the one of the last things I tell myself each night. I follow that with Jewish prayers, positive affirmations, and reflections on things for which I am grateful. I fall back to sleep quickly, and I sleep in peace, knowing that I am exactly where I need to be.

February 3, 2022

Chapter Forty-Three

Plant a Tree to Save the World

*"See to it that you do not spoil and destroy My world; for if you do,
there will be no one else to repair it.'"
(Midrash Kohelet Rabbah, 1 on Ecclesiastes 7:13)*

Would you like to do your part to save our planet in a meaningful way? Plant a tree—or two—or be part of the Trillion Tree Campaign. No matter how many you plant, you will be doing your part for the environment.

Although there are still doubters, climate change is a real threat to our future. According to the United Nations' Intergovernmental Panel on Climate Change, the world has 11 years to take dramatic policy action and shift away from fossil fuels to avoid the worst effects of climate change. Reports like that keep me up at night.

In his 2019 book *Falter: Has the Human Game Begun to Play Itself Out?* Bill McKibbon describes the present as a bleak moment in human history. He states that we will either confront that bleakness or watch the civilization our forebears built slip away. Okay, that information keeps me up at night AND gives me nightmares!

I can despair, or I can act. As a Jew, I am called to the social justice theology of *Tikkun Olam*, the perfecting or the repairing of the world. This principle keeps me strongly anchored to my religion. Full disclosure: When I attend services, I love the music and the flow of the prayers. Often, however, prayers that praise God are not as important to me as prayers that call me to action. And some holidays call us to action more than others. One such holiday is *Tu B'Shvat*. For those of us who care deeply about the future of our planet, this holiday which celebrates the "New Year for Trees," offers a Jewish connection to contemporary ecological issues. Modern Jews view the holiday as the opportunity to educate Jews about their tradition's advocacy of responsible stewardship of God's creation, manifested in ecological activism.

And one such way is to plant trees. Many American and European Jews observe Tu BShvat by contributing money to the Jewish National Fund, an organization devoted to reforesting Israel. Founded in 1901 to buy and develop land in what was then the Ottoman Palestine, the JNF has planted over 240 million trees in Israel along with other environmental achievements including the building and development of dams, reservoirs, and parks.

More recently, planting trees has taken on a global focus. Inspired by Wangari Maathai, founder of the Green Belt Movement whose goal included organizing women in rural Kenya to plant trees, the Trillion Tree Campaign has already resulted in the planting of 13.6 billion trees in 193 countries.

According to a study released by Dr. Thomas Crowther and fellow scientists at ETH Zurich, a Swiss university, planting billions of trees across the world is one of the most available and least expensive way of taking CO_2 out of the atmosphere to tackle the climate crisis. As trees grow, they absorb and store the carbon dioxide emissions that are driving global heating. New research estimates that a worldwide planting program could remove two-thirds of all the emissions from human activities that remain in the atmosphere today.

I am not naive enough to believe that my making contributions to JNF or other agencies committed to reforestation will single-handedly solve the climate crisis. I will do my best to further reduce my carbon footprint by driving a hybrid car, bundling errands that require driving to use the least amount of fuel, and using energy-efficient appliances and light bulbs. I will continue to recycle despite changes in recent policies in many areas that limit what we can put in our bins. (I still feel guilty every time I throw plastic and glass containers in the garbage!) I will continue to read, study, write and advocate for the environment. And I will vote for politicians who share my concerns for our planet.

"It's the little things citizens do. That's what will make the difference," stated Maathai, who won the Nobel Peace Prize in 2004 for her environmental efforts. "My little thing is planting trees." If we can choose to do our own "little thing," we may be able to keep our planet healthy. After all, as expressed in a popular meme, there is no Planet B.

February 6, 2021; Updated for this book.

134

Chapter Forty-Four

Purim: Shiker or Sober?

Purim is around the corner, and not far behind are costumes and dancing and Purim shpiels and groggers and hamantashen.

And, for some, alcohol. According to the Talmud, it is one's duty, to "make oneself fragrant [with wine] on Purim until one cannot tell the difference between Haman and Mordecai."(Babylonian Talmud, Megillah 7b). On this one holiday, alcohol is not the most important element, but many imbibe. As explained by writer Tvi Freeman, Purim is not about drinking. It about being drunk with happiness that, despite Haman's attempt to totally annihilate the Jewish people, Jews stood up to evil and won. Rational? Logical? No, but we managed to survive.

Getting physically drunk on Purim has not been one of my own memories. I always have tied the holiday to children and often, at least in my synagogues, some kind of cheesy fair that involved parent-made booths and dime-store prizes. The first adult Purim party I attended was one held by the Capital District Jewish Singles on March 18, 1973, where I met my future husband, Larry. That was the best prize I could have won. That party, held on the second floor of Herbie's Restaurant, did not involve alcohol either.

Jews may drink a glass of wine on Shabbat; the number goes up to four on Passover. We are encouraged to drink on *Simchas Torah*, the holiday that celebrates and marks the conclusion of the annual cycle of public Torah readings and the beginning of a new cycle. Copious alcohol consumption never was a "Jewish" thing. In fact, statistically, Jews have less of a chance of becoming alcoholics than other demographics.

Why? The first reason is genetics. According to a 2002 study done at Columbia University, many Jews—nearly 20%—have a DNA mutation linked to lower rates of alcoholism. The variance, say scientists, known as ADH2*2, is involved in the way the body breaks down alcohol in the bloodstream and is thought to produce more of a toxic chemical by-product when persons with the gene drink heavily.

Another reason is culture. In a 2014 article in *Sh'ma: A Journal of Jewish Ideas,* alcohol counselor Lew Weiss writes that even though many Jewish traditions involve alcohol, Jews condemn actual drunkenness. The fear of being ostracized by their peers results in fewer Jews with drinking problems. And if they do, they are less likely to come out of the closet.

A third reason deals with the Jews' drink of choice. In a 1980 study out of Syracuse University, Jews tend to drink wine more often than any other group and—at least forty years ago—few alcohol abusers concentrated on wine.

While growing up in Upstate New York, I rarely saw my parents or relatives drink alcohol. Family gatherings never included beer, hard liquor, or even wine. To this day, I can't picture even having kept beer in the refrigerator, but we must have. When I was twelve, my father asked me to get two beers for him and a friend who was visiting. I grabbed the bottles from the frig, filled up two tall glasses with ice, and watched in horror as the Schlitz or Genesee foamed all over the counter. Hey! That's what we did with soda, right?

Two of our family stories involved my mother's unknowing encounter with alcohol. In 1955, my mother, who was five months pregnant with my younger sister, drank several glasses of what she thought was a delicious red fruit punch at a local Kiwanis get-together. When the president asked everyone to rise for the pledge of allegiance, my mother stood up, put her hand over her heart, and promptly fainted. She came to on a couch with our family doctor, who was fortunately in attendance, by her side. "Young lady," said Dr. Temple sternly, "you should not be drinking so much alcohol, especially in your delicate condition!"

The second story came from my mother and father's decision to follow our Uncle Paul's recipe for cherry brandy. As the big jar of the fresh fruit soaked up the vodka/sugar mixture, my mother helped herself to one or two of the cherries the first day, three or four the next, six the next. That night, my father came home to dinner and a tipsy wife. "It's just fruit!" she cried. No more cherries for my mother!

Like my mother, I naively fell prey to another delicious red fruit punch. I started Albany State one week after my eighteenth birthday and had no experience with recreational drinking as I was a tea-totaler/good girl throughout high school. On my first date, my older companion, an exchange student from Russian, recommended that I order a Singapore sling. Two tall glasses of sweet mixture of cherry brandy, gin, and fruit juices put me on my proverbial *tuches*. From then on, I stuck to less potent combinations.

Another of my learning experiences occurred after I graduated college. In June 1973, I attended my cousin Marsha's wedding in Richfield Springs, New York. I was getting over bronchitis and took my dose of cough medicine with codeine with breakfast. Six hours later, after a long drive and the wedding ceremony, I quickly downed two alcoholic drinks from the open bar on an empty stomach. Were they screwdrivers? Whiskey sours? It didn't matter. The combination of booze and codeine resulted in a giant hangover that left me in bed in the dark with cold compresses on my head for two days. I stupidly hadn't realized the danger of mixing prescription drugs and alcohol. Years later, I found out such a toxic combination put Karen Ann Quinlan into a coma and subsequent vegetative state that triggered the historic right-to-die fight that ended up in the Supreme Court.

Larry and I enjoy a glass of wine or beer—Guinness or Sam Adams for Larry and a Blue Moon with a slice of orange for me. To be honest, I think I enjoy the citrus more than the beer. Larry and I have relaxed a bit on vacation—especially at the all-inclusive resort we used to visit in Jamaica. At Grand Lido Braco, I discovered a wonderful hazelnut liquor, so much so that I earned the moniker "Sister Frangelica" from my fellow Caribbean travelers. At Grand Lido Negril, Larry and our friend Jim discovered chocolate martinis, which he refers to as chocolate milk for adults. The Caribbean influence shows up in another one of our favorites: coconut rum and Coke.

Purim or not, the pandemic had a definite effect on our drinking. In the early months, our routine included a nightly "Happy Hour," which consisted of a glass of wine, our rum and coke, or a beer. That was severely curbed, however, when my routine blood tests, which are usually stellar, came back with a slight elevation in my liver enzymes. My doctor gently suggested cutting back on my alcohol consumption. Now, except for an occasional splurge, my version of a "strong drink" is a glass of club soda with lemon and three maraschino cherries—just not the brandy-infused fruit to which my mom fell prey.

That is fine with me. Any adult beverages, especially mixed drinks loaded with sugar, have always been wasted on me. I drink them too fast, slurping the bottom of my glass before my fellow drinkers have hardly started. I'd rather put those calories toward a huge dish of vanilla ice cream.

On the evening of March 14, our synagogue is having a Purim party. There will be costumes and dancing and a Purim *shpiel* and groggers and hamantashen. No alcohol, though, just soda and some iced tea. I know that no one will even notice or care. We will be *shiker*, drunk with happiness that Jews, despite all of those who tried to annihilate us, have survived.

March 15, 2022

Chapter Forty-Five

Lifetime Achievement Awards

For the past two years, Passover has—well—passed over us. In 2020, Larry and I had a seder for two, a quiet affair to say the least. In 2021, thanks to Zoom, we were at least able to share a *Haggadah* and the holiday with members of our synagogue.

Now we are back in the game. Our first night will not be that much different, in that our congregation has opted for a Zoom service for hopefully the last time. But on the second night, we will drive to Sarasota, where we will share a table with two of my siblings and their spouses. It will be lovely to sip wine and eat matzah and charotzes with family.

And, as always, I am entering this holiday with the same feeling of gratitude I have managed to maintain since COVID-19 closed down our world. True, Larry and I have missed much—especially a year away from our children and their families. We spent two years avoiding crowds, passing up on movies and plays, getting our boosters and wearing masks. But I feel that the worst parts of this pandemic have passed over us. It is as if our doorposts were marked with a blessing that prevented illness and sadness from touching so many that we love.

We may not have suffered all the effects of this scourge, but we have unfortunately not escaped from another inevitable issue: Aging! In a recent article in the *New Yorker* article, David Kemp suggests that his newly formed US Citizens for Age Forgiveness demand an "executive order that will decree the last two years do not count toward the age of an American."

Of course, Kemp's essay is tongue in cheek, but I agree. Any setbacks that were caused by almost two years of hunkering down should somehow be erased and given back to us as a gift from God. This is especially true regarding what Larry has affectionally called "Lifetime Achievement Awards," all those hopefully bearable inconveniences that are a result of surviving into our 60s and 70s.

First example: Cataracts. I cannot turn around without bumping into someone who is in some stage of this common eye surgery. Conversations revolve around which doctor to use; which version of the lens to be implanted from the no-frills basic to the top-of-the line deluxe; which drops therapy is used, how long between Eye One and Eye Two; and how long one can return to normal life. We have come to accept the fact that people are walking around with one lens popped out of their glasses, not exactly a Lens Crafter advertisement.

Unlike other surgeries, there is a definite benefit. After years of dealing with glasses and contact lenses, we Baby Boomers are looking at the world through our own eyes. My own journey to cataract surgery goes back almost 20 years ago when I spoke to my eye doctor about getting Lasik surgery to repair my severe myopia. He suggested I wait. "Most people of a certain age [Notice he kindly avoided the word 'old.'] require cataract surgery," he told me. "I can almost promise you will get the vision you want without the expense if you just wait it out." He was correct. I patiently waited until my cataracts, first imperceptible, then ripening, then, in my mid 60s, were ready to fix. My glasses went to the Lions Club, and my contact lenses and all the required accessories went into the trash. It took me months to break myself of the habit of reaching for my glasses the minute I woke up. To this day, if I feel something in my eye, my first thought is that something is lurking under my contacts.

Because I had been wearing contacts since I was in my 20s, my appearance didn't change after surgery. Larry, however, had been wearing glasses for over 30 years until his recent surgery. I am still getting used to the "bare nakedness" of my un-bespectacled mate. So is my granddaughter, who burst into tears when she saw her Zayde for the first time without his usually dark frames. My sister-in-law Leslie was grateful that she still needed to wear glasses after cataract surgery. "I like myself better with glasses," she told me. "They hide the wrinkles"

Eyes are not the only body part that falls under the "Lifetime Achievement Award" category. Many of our teeth, which at one point held under the strain of carrots, popcorn, and even hard candy, seem to be crumbling, resulting in crowns, implants, and bridges. Hips, shoulders, and knees are also being replaced at an alarming rate. Some of us have so many fake parts we rival Lee Majors' Bionic Man.

Unfortunately, the standard devices do not imbue their owners with any superpower, including super hearing. As a matter of fact, based on the number of ads for hearing aids found in AARP magazine, the inability to pick up normal conversations is one of the most prevalent signs of our aging bodies. Both Larry and I are on the cusp of needing some help. We can no longer have a conversation when we are in two different rooms. Heck, we have problems hearing each other when we are sitting side by side on the couch doing crossword puzzles.

"What did you get for 41 across?" Larry recently asked me.

"Heeded," I answered.

"Needed? It doesn't fit. 33 down is OG**H**."

I said '**H**eeded.'"

"**S**eeded?"

"No! **H**eeded. **H** as in Harry!"

"As in **L**arry?"

139

No wonder it is taking us longer to do these puzzles.

A friend's Pilates instructor had a different, but still flattering, spin on her geriatric gym rats. She regards us as "classic cars," older, still viable, very much appreciated, even if we are restored.

Unfortunately, Lifetime Achievement Awards often come in more serious forms. Cancers. Heart problems. Diabetes. Cognitive issues. Family and friends are dealing with many of these issues, a result of living a long life or of just plain bad luck.

A recent broadcast on NPR stated that with key COVID-19 metrics trending rapidly downward, the pandemic's third spring is already looking very different. Passover 5782 will hopefully usher in a time of hope that COVID-19 will be, if not conquered, at least controlled. I also wish that this be a time of a *refuah shlema,* a complete, speedy healing for those suffering from all those lifetime achievement awards. And as we gather at our more crowded seder table, let us add Rabbi Naomi Levy's pandemic-inspired prayer: "On this Passover Night/We pray to you, God/Let it Pass Over us/Hear us, God/Heal us, God. Amen."

March 31, 2022

Chapter Forty-Six

First World Problems

We all go through periods which feel as if a cloud has settled over our heads. I certainly can attest that at times I have felt like Ziggy, the iconic comic strip character.

Our troubles began with a home remodel. Tired of the original orangey-brown pseudo-oak cabinets in our kitchen, I convinced Larry that refacing them in white would be worth the time and money. When the company's time frame to do the work coincided with my planned trip to Colorado, Larry graciously turned down my suggestions to delay the work until I returned. He would handle the last couple of days of installation and most of the clean-up on his own.

The weekend before my departure, Larry and I emptied out the entire contents of our cabinets into our living/dining room. When I attempted to run one last load of dishes before we had to close the kitchen for the next few days, the door on our dishwasher fell down with a thud, almost taking out my knee. The door springs had unsprung.

My washing machine must have decided it would have sympathy pains. Less than an hour later, I attempted to run a load of laundry. In the middle of the cycle, the machine stopped, and all sorts of lights began flashing. An internet search informed us that it was either a lid latch ($) or motherboard ($$$) malfunction. We threw the soaked clothes into our fairly new dryer—the old one had died in November. First thing Monday morning, as the crew descended on our kitchen to begin work, I made a phone call to an appliance repair company to repair the dishwasher door and washing machine latch.

Unfortunately, the appliance people couldn't help me with the crown on my back molar that had fallen off that morning while I was flossing my teeth. And the dentist would have to wait, as I didn't have time to get to his office before my trip. I stuck it back on and hoped for the best.

After driving me to the airport Wednesday, Larry returned to a torn-up kitchen sealed off in plastic and a house filled with the overwhelming smell of paint. Meanwhile, my attempt at self-dentistry only lasted until I bit into an ice cream cone I had grabbed at the airport while waiting for the shuttle to take me to my daughter's house. An emergency trip to her dentist was for naught. After a valiant, 45-minute attempt to glue the sucker back on, the dentist gave up and recommended I think about pulling out the remains of the tooth when I returned home.

Meanwhile, back in Florida, the appliance repairman was one for two: the dishwasher was an easy fix, but the washing machine's motherboard was gone. Larry and I spent an hour on the phone choosing a new machine from a local hardware store's website. While I was hiking with my family on a beautiful Saturday in the Rockies, Larry was waiting for the new machine to arrive. No worries. He had plenty to do in the meantime as the kitchen work was completed. Larry put most of the kitchenware back into the new cabinets, leaving the spice drawers and some other cabinets for me to organize to my liking. Yes, I married a gem!

I returned Tuesday night, and by Wednesday afternoon, the kitchen was completely back in business—or maybe not. Our nine-year-old refrigerator was not only freezing the ice cream but also the eggs, milk, lettuce, and grapes. We made another call to the appliance man. Repairs could run up to $500, he told us. Maybe we should consider just biting the bullet and getting a new one? Another run to the appliance store, another swish of the credit card, and we only had to live with frozen foods for a little while longer.

On the scheduled delivery day, I got a call saying the truck delivering our new side-by-side would be there in thirty minutes. This gave me just enough time to move the contents of the old refrigerator into laundry baskets and boxes commandeered for the project. When the deliverymen arrived, they pulled out their tape measures, stretched them across our front door, and shook their heads. "Sorry. Doesn't look like your new frig will fit through the door." Some quick problem-solving resulted in a "through-the-lanai-if-we-dislodge-the-screen-door" option. An hour later, the old frig was in the truck and the new one was sitting in the middle of a kitchen filled with warming and—worst yet—melting food.

"The new hose for the ice maker doesn't work. Wrong clamp," Roy explained from the back of the machine. "I'll attach the old one."

"As long as it works, I'm fine with that," I said.

Ten minutes later, the refrigerator was ready for the final push into place.

"It's too wide," said Roy. "I can't get it into the space."

"Just remove the molding," I suggested.

"We don't do that," Roy informed me.

"You are not leaving here until that refrigerator is installed," I said between gritted-minus-one-uncapped-molar tooth. "If I have to, *I* will remove the damn molding!"

Roy shrugged and tried one more push. Miraculously, it squeaked in with centimeters to spare. Whew! After two hours of work, these guys deserved a tip, which I gave willingly.

Now let *me* offer a tip. Before the appliance people leave you with your new refrigerator, check to see if the ice maker and water dispenser work. In the end, we had to pay an outside plumber to do that job. And did I mention that our *new* refrigerator also froze our food? (That was replaced with one that sounded like a dentist's drill until that was finally fixed.)

All the fails joined the Mr. Coffee, microwave, Ninja blender, electric tea kettle, toaster oven, and aforementioned clothes dryer that had all died in a six-month period. How many appliances did I have left to replace? To add to the mix, I blew out two electrical outlets when I saturated a power strip while washing down our lanai floor with a hose.

The following week, Larry and I welcomed Chris and Bernie, old friends whom we hadn't seen since the beginning of the pandemic, The four of us celebrated our reunion by enjoying a delicious dinner at a local Asian restaurant.

As we were waiting for our waiter to return with our receipts, Chris noted that we hadn't gotten any fortune cookies. "No problem!" I said. I walked up to the basket of cookies next to the cash register, grabbed four at random, and dropped them on our table. Mine read "GO FOR THE GOLD TODAY! YOU'LL BE THE CHAMPION OF WHATEVER!"

After all that had happened to us over the previous couple of weeks, I was pretty happy to get this fortune. As I shared it with everyone, I proclaimed, "A sign! My luck is changing!"

As I was saying this, our waiter Ben came by with the receipt and four more fortune cookies. When he saw we already had them, Ben suggested that these might be even better. I opened mine, only to read "IGNORE PREVIOUS COOKIE."

In the scheme of things, these are all First World Problems. I only need to hear about another friend's illness, read the latest headlines, or see another heart-wrenching picture from the Ukraine to remind myself that, as Rick tells Ilsa in the last moments of *Casablanca*," Our problems don't amount to a hill of beans in this crazy world." A wise woman once told me, "If it can be [legally] fixed with money, consider yourself lucky." We are grateful that we only have had to deal for a short time with unwashed clothes, dangerous doors, frozen eggs, dentist drills, or unfortunate fortune cookies.

April 14, 2022

Chapter Forty-Seven

Pickleball *Putz*

I am a proud pickleball dropout. After a brief attempt to learn the game from Larry, I realized that being interested in something and having enough talent to play on the most basic level are two different things.

What? You haven't heard of pickleball? Have you been living under a marinated mushroom? According to the 2022 Sports & Fitness Industry Association (SFIA), there are 4.8 million people who play the game in the United States alone. It is the fastest growing sport in the country.

Until Larry and I retired, I myself had never heard about pickleball. Larry had been involved in sports his entire life—basketball, baseball, and track in his youth, and running and cycling as an adult. When he turned 65, we both joined the local YMCA. While I took classes and swam laps in the Olympic-sized pool, Larry started playing pickleball with friends from Congregation Beth Shalom and other members of the Y.

Both competitive and athletic, Larry fell in love with the game immediately. He found camaraderie as well as the ability—to quote Jimmy Buffet—"to grow older but not up."

When we moved to Florida, one of the conditions for where we would live was contingent upon having aerobic classes and a lap pool for me and having pickleball courts for Larry. We both found what we were looking for in Solivita, our 55+ active adult community. Larry joined the Smashers and found players at his level. To make his life even better, Larry found the Summit County Pickleball Club ("We play with altitude!") near where we rent in Colorado every summer.

Larry sat out on pickleball for the first year of the pandemic. He missed it, however, and justified his returning to the courts. "I'll be outside, and there is plenty of hand sanitizer and even a bucket with an alcohol base in which I can wash the balls." I was still concerned, but we compromised. I would continue biking but would resume my trips to the pool. I justified my pool time as well. "The chlorine will kill all the coronavirus germs," I reassured myself.

Pickleball not only provided Larry with a great form of exercise, but it also provided a social outlet. In Florida, the Smashers had dances and breakfasts; in Colorado, the players had potlucks and happy hours. As a matter of fact, it was the social aspect of "pb'ing" at 9100 feet that got my interest. Larry was playing the game at least four mornings a week, and he was meeting lots of people. I, on the other hand, spent my mornings either hiking by myself or with my grand dog or, occasionally, swimming lonely laps in a pool that accepted Silver Sneakers. Maybe learning the game would help me become part of a community.

One sunny day, I asked Larry to take me onto the Colorado courts during a time set aside for beginners interested in trying the game. After giving me some of the basic rules, Larry gently lobbed me a ball; I hit it. Hey! This wasn't so bad! Slow lob, hit. Slow lob. "I got this!" I thought.

When he started hitting the balls to me at the normal rate of speed, however, I could barely connect with the ball. Only 30 minutes into my private lesson, a slim, athletic couple came onto the court.

"We'd love some lessons, too!" they said. Larry quickly repeated some of the basics, and the two of them took to it like "white on rice." At that point, they told us they had been playing tennis their whole lives, so this was an easy transition. Larry then suggested the four of us play a game together.

Now it was a completely different game. Fast lob, Marilyn miss. Fast lob, Marilyn miss. Soon Larry was covering both sides of our court to cover for me.

You have to understand that I wasn't even close to hitting the ball. My lifetime lack of hand-eye coordination, exacerbated by vision problems brought on by age, resulted in my swinging at lots of air. The ball was usually two feet above or two feet below my pathetic paddle.

So, I did what any normal, mature adult would do in that situation. I told Larry I didn't want to play anymore, went back to our car, sat in the front seat, and cried.

"I can't do it," I told Larry after he finished his session with the two tennis pros. "I hate it! I can't see the ball. I can't hit the ball. I can't even move in time. I'm done."

I was. And I am. I am in the eighth decade of my life. Up until now, I had proven myself lousy at tennis and baseball and racquetball and squash, I have now proved myself to be lousy at pickleball. The benefits of being part of a large group—there are at least 1000 members of Smashers—are totally outweighed by how much I hate trying to hit a stupid ball with a stupid paddle that may result in my breaking a stupid bone.

"You should try playing with us," some friends have told me. "None of us play that well, and we won't care if you're not great at it." "No thanks," I tell them. "I'd rather walk or swim or bike or do an exercise class."

And after hearing about all my friends with pickleball-related injuries, I am happy to stick to what I am doing. None of them require hand/eye coordination. None of them are competitive, so I don't have to always lose. Better yet, I won't be the player that no one wants on their team. Yes, my short stint as a pickleball *putz* is over! From now on, my only pickle of choice is a kosher one in a jar.

May 2, 2022

This story was also published by *Chicken Soup for the Soul* under "Well, That was Funny," Amy Newmark, editor. 2023

Chapter Forty-Eight

Say Yes To The Wrong Dress

Adam had his first date with Sarah on December 25, 2018. They got engaged on June 23, 2019. By the time Larry and I met Carol and Dick, Sarah's parents, in August, they had the rabbi, the October date, the venue, the DJ, and the photographer all lined up. All that was left to do was for them to send out the invitations and for all of us to figure out what we would be wearing.

In August, Sarah found a beautiful long sleeve white lace dress. At the same store, Carol and Sarah's sister Molly found their dresses; a long gold brocade for Carol and a black off-the shoulder top with a lovely, flowered pattern for Molly. Julie purchased a beautiful teal green dress on E-Bay, the same place she had found her wedding dress twelve years before.

When Sarah and Adam asked our granddaughter to be flower girl, the Mountain Girl was thrilled—and prepared. "I will wear my Elsa dress," she announced. Julie gently explained that rather than her *Frozen* costume, Mommy would be buying her a *special* dress for her important role in the wedding. "Okay," she said. "I will save the Elsa dress for MY wedding!"

Like my granddaughter, I originally planned on wearing a dress I already owned. I had purchased a cocktail dress the previous December for our community's Shalom Club Ball. It was my favorite color, midnight blue, and the V-neck sleeveless design fell perfectly on mid-knee. When I shared my decision with my mah-jongg group, they objected.

"Your son only gets married once," said Sharon, who led the charge. "You have been waiting a very long time for this! Get a new dress!"

Soon after this discussion, Larry and I celebrated our 45th anniversary by going out to dinner at a restaurant in one of Orlando's largest shopping centers. I suggested to Larry that we leave early so that we could look at suits for him (Adam and Sam had already purchased new suits) and at dresses for me.

When we perused the men's department at Macy's, Larry refused to even try on a suit. "I don't need a new one," he said. "The one I have in the closet is fine." His only concession was to agree to have a tailor remove the pants' cuffs, definitely no longer in style.

I had better luck—or maybe a better attitude—in the women's department. After several fails, I tried on a more sophisticated version of the midnight blue dress I had worn to the Shalom Club Ball. Sleeveless with a diagonal neckline, it had a beautiful silver brooch on the right side. The saleslady who was helping me agreed that was perfect for the evening event. She suggested it would look even better if I also invested in some (expensive) shapewear that would smooth out some of my bumps and lumps. As the chances of losing twenty pounds by the wedding were slim, I agreed. Okay, the dress wasn't a Size 10, but when I pulled the whole thing together—I looked pretty amazing, and Larry agreed.

I asked the salesperson to snap a picture on my iPhone, which I sent to my mah-jongg group. Within minutes, my phone was dinging like crazy.

"Yay! You are going to look gorgeousssss!"

"You are one SEXY MAMA! Don't play safe! Go for bold & sexy!"

"You go girl!"

Then the text messages took on a life of their own, where I became the topic of discussion. "She needs shoes to match the dress."

"[Hair] updo would make her look better."

"She needs new makeup."

This discussion continued the following Friday at mah-jongg. One by one, my fairy god sisters helped me accessorize by shopping in their closets. Beautiful silver sandals. A glittery handbag. A midnight blue bracelet. Sapphire hanging earrings.

They had one more suggestion—a trip to Sephora. After a first class make-over, I dropped over $100 on makeup, including foundation, blush, and an eye shadow palette with some silver glitter. I was set!

I wasn't going to risk a chance of losing the outfit on our flight out to San Francisco. So, three days before we left, I packed everything I needed in my carry-on. I carefully placed the plastic clothing bag protecting the dress on top of the shoes, handbag, and undergarments. Fortunately, there were no flight problems on our way out, and I hung the entire outfit in our hotel room closet.

That evening, Larry and I met Adam and Sarah for dinner. To our surprise, Sarah showed us Wedding Dress Number Two. She felt the simple white sheath reflected more of her personality than the original Seventies design. Besides, Wedding Dress Number One was no longer an option, as our future grandchild—a boy!—was making his presence known.

The days leading up to the wedding were a whirlwind of total happiness and joy. Friends and relatives flew in from around the country. Many took advantage of the beautiful weather and the San Francisco location to tour the area. The night before the wedding, Larry and I hosted a welcome dinner at Sarah's parents 'home,

The morning of the wedding, my siblings and I took a bus tour of San Francisco while Larry and Adam had professional shaves. We all got back to the hotel in plenty of time to get ready. I put on my new makeup, spent a little more time on my hair, slipped on my shape wear, buckled up my beautiful silver sandals, put on my sapphire earrings and bracelet, took the dress out of the plastic bag, and slipped it over my head.

"Larry, would you please zip me up?"

Larry finished knotting his tie and turned his attention to me.

"Marilyn, that is NOT the dress you bought for the wedding," Larry said. "That is the Shalom Club Ball dress."

I looked in the mirror. He was right. After all that, I had packed the WRONG dress. Not the dress I bought for the wedding and had spent three weeks accessorizing. Nope, it was the dress I originally was going to wear.

"I can't believe I brought the wrong dress!" I cried. "I can't believe I brought the wrong dress!"

In ten minutes, the Uber was coming to pick us up. There was no way in the world I could fly back to Florida and grab the right one. I shook my head and accepted the inevitable.

"I guess I will be wearing this dress to the wedding!" Fortunately, both were midnight blue with silver accents. The only touch needed was a necklace to fit into the V-neck of the dress. Fortunately, my niece Laura had brought a sapphire and diamond necklace on a silver chain. Perfect!

When Larry and I arrived at the wedding venue, we saw Sarah in her beautiful Wedding Dress Number Two and Adam in his new suit. Soon after, Carol and Dick Nathan, Sarah's parents, came to the restaurant. Rather than wearing the dress she had purchased in August, Carol decided to wear the dress her own mother had worn at Carol and Dick's wedding 48 years before.

Julie, Sam, and The Mountain Girl came in next. My granddaughter looked like a fairy princess in her pink and white flower girl dress and flower garland. The only people wearing their first choices were Julie and Molly

and the rest of the men, including Larry, whose old suit was perfect for the occasion.

To say Adam and Sarah's wedding was special was the understatement of the year. I may have brought the wrong dress. As they approach their third anniversary, Sarah has proven again and again that Adam, more importantly, has married the right person—a smart, caring, independent woman who is beautiful inside and out. And, in the end, that is all that matters.

And the "right" dress? Outside of wearing it to a Hanukkah Ball in our community in December 2019, the original Adam/Sarah's wedding dress hung in my closet for almost three years. In August 2022, I finally had the opportunity to wear it to our nephew's Massachusetts wedding. As it was an outdoor affair, the fancy shoes were replaced with a pair of flats. And the shapewear? The pandemic has taught me a great deal, including comfort outweighs any attempt in concealing my curves. And I fit right in.

Originally published October 19, 2019.
Updated for this book.

Chapter Forty-Nine

Happy Wherever I Am

There is always, always something to be thankful for.
Author unknown

When Julie headed out to Colorado in 2003, it was originally planned as a nine-month adventure teaching environmental science. Soon, however, Julie fell in love with the Rockies, Colorado, and Sam, not necessarily in that order. They built a life together, completed graduate degrees, got married, bought a house in Frisco, and had a child. They have settled into life at 9100 feet.

Meanwhile, Adam chose a different path in another Frisco...San Francisco. After completing a law degree, he moved into an apartment in the middle of the city. In December 2018, he met Sarah. In a whirlwind romance, they dated, got engaged, got married, and are now the parents of two children. They have settled into life at sea level.

In the middle of all this, Larry and I decided to move from Upstate New York to a fifty-five plus community in Florida, close to 2000 and 3000 miles from Frisco and San Francisco, respectively. There are those who ask us when we are moving closer to our children. The answer is "not now."

Feeling gratitude despite living so far away may be difficult to fathom. However, I am thankful. Both my children have chosen to settle in two of the most wonderful places we have ever visited. Recent experiences bear that out.

Frisco, Colorado is nestled in beautiful Summit County. Surrounded by mountains reaching over 14,000 feet, it is for us a summer wonderland. Trails beckon us on hikes that bring us next to flowing streams, stunning wildflowers, and expansive vista. Larry plays with the Summit County pickleball league while I take long walks with my grand dog. Free concerts are offered in most surrounding towns Thursdays through Sunday.

Our favorite concert is the one on Main Street in Frisco every week. Hundreds of people congregate around the pavilion in the middle of Frisco Town Park. The adults settle into lawn chairs and on blankets, pulling dinners out of coolers, while their dogs settle nearby. Meanwhile, the children dart around the lawn and path around the pavilion. It is a slice of Americana that I hadn't seen since growing up in our Upstate New York town. In addition to the free entertainment, the area has several theater groups and a summer residency for the National Repertory Orchestra. And the hiking! Our condo is a stone's throw away from trails that can take us to Breckinridge in one direction and Vail in another. Since our granddaughter was born, we have rented a condo for several weeks each summer, taking in all the beauty and helping out with childcare.

One thousand miles away, San Francisco is one of the most beloved cities in America. When we visit Adam and his family, we have taken advantage of all its attractions. We have walked through Golden Gate Park and across the iconic bridge. We have visited Alcatraz, Muir Woods, Sausalito, and Point del Reyes. We have watched the massive Gay Pride parade. We have used the city as a starting point to attractions as far south as Monterey and as far north as Astoria, Oregon.

With such wonderful places to go, why have we have not picked up and moved again?

This question has taken on new meaning now that we have a granddaughter in Colorado and two grandchildren in San Francisco.

Let me start with Frisco. Everything I wrote about my favorite town in the world is during the summer. Its year-round residents can experience snow through June, enjoy a beautiful but brief summer, and see the first dusting of snow on nearby ski resorts by mid-September. When we visited Julie and Sam one mid-October, snow fell on five out of six days.

As an Upstate New York girl, I always loved the sight of clean, white snow on lawns and trees and trails. Unfortunately, sidewalks are not immune. After dropping The Mountain Girl at pre-school the second full day we were there, the sun was shining everywhere, including on the black ice on the sidewalks. In the end, we had to leave for the airport a day early as a major storm was expected to bring hazardous conditions to Route 70. The Weather Channel advisory recommended travelers to pack food, water, and blankets in case one was stranded. Although the snowfall never amounted to more than 2 inches (Denver actually got more!), the temperature dipped to 16 degrees above zero, without windchill. We love Frisco but cannot see us living there through their long winters.

The weather in Adam and Sarah's now established hometown is admittedly better. Even if you factor in the famous Mark Twain quote, "The coldest winter I ever spent was a summer in San Francisco," we would never have to deal with snow. The city, however, is known for its steep hills and even steeper housing prices. If we sold our home in Florida, we could possibly afford a bathroom. No, I am not talking about a one bedroom, one bath apartment. I am talking about a bathroom. No shower included. And to get to that bathroom, we would probably have to walk up four flights of stairs, as the natives seem to eschew elevators.

Here are two more reasons not to move. First of all, a number of friends have relocated to be close to their children, only to see their offspring relocate one or two years later because of their careers.

Finally, Larry and I love where we are. We are in a one-floor home that is a perfect size for the two of us. Our 55+ community offers activities that fit our needs: pickleball courts; fully equipped gyms, Olympic-sized pools, restaurants, and entertainment venues. To add to our pleasure, we have our choice of over 250 clubs and organizations with which to participate within our gates. Within a forty-minute drive, we have all that Orlando has to offer, including world class entertainment and Disney.

We were especially grateful for our Florida home during the pandemic. Yes, we missed not being able to see our family so far away, and the sweltering summer of 2020 was brutal. But Larry and I were able to take long walks and longer bike rides. One of the eleven smaller neighborhood pools became our go-to spot after exercise. Most of the time, no more than six of us were in the pool, playing games supplied by a former physical education teacher. Once we felt safer, we were able to resume social events held outdoors even in the "winter" months when the temperatures dropped to a "frigid" 50 degrees.

So, we are here to stay for as long as we can maintain our independent lifestyle. We are grateful that both our children have chosen to settle in two of the most wonderful places we have ever experienced. Even more so after the pandemic curtailed numerous trips, we have planned visits as well as a promise to them that we can be on a plane in a moment's notice if needed. Meanwhile, the guest room is ready for them anytime.

Originally written November 29, 2019.
Updated for this book.

Chapter Fifty

No Escape

Guess who contracted COVID-19?

After months and months of being careful, I had pressed my luck. As Special Olympics Track and Field coaches, Larry and I attended the Florida State Special Olympics games with eleven athletes from our county on May 20 and 21, 2022. All our events, which took place in the ESPN Wide World of Sports Complex in Orlando, were supposed to be outdoors. Plans changed quickly when torrential rains and strong winds swept in moments after we had parked our car. Our team, along with several other teams from a variety of sports, spent the first two hours sheltering in the Advent Health Building lobby. The "close encounters of the super-spreading kind" happened again that night when rain delayed and then finally resulted in the cancellation of opening ceremonies. Although Larry opted not to wear a mask, I made sure I had my KN95 covering my face whenever I was inside. Outside, however, I eschewed protection, hoping for the best.

Fortunately, the weather improved the second day of competition. By Saturday afternoon, however, I was exhausted. I tried to hydrate, but I was totally wiped. *Maybe I'm getting too old for this,* I thought to myself. Or maybe I was just feeling the effects of two sleep-deprived nights, two mornings of 6 a.m. alarms, and putting on at least eight miles corralling our athletes to various venues in 90-degree heat and 90% humidity.

By the time our last athlete had claimed his second-place medal in the 400-meter walk, even Larry, who had shown no signs of slowing down, was ready to get out of the heat and go home. We stopped for a late lunch, drove home and collapsed on our couch. After a slow walk on Sunday morning, we went to Publix for our second booster shot. Then we spent the rest of Sunday with a repeat performance on the couch.

On Monday, I attempted my usual walk but felt as if I were plowing through mud. By Tuesday afternoon, exhaustion was accompanied by congestion and a runny nose. "Just a head cold," I thought. It took me until Wednesday to administer the home test.

You know how it usually takes 15 minutes to see the results? Forget that. Within thirty-seconds of putting the disgusting drops into the assigned spot on the test strip, the "positive" line showed up.

"I have COVID," I texted Larry, who was at a ROMEO [Retired Old Men Eating Out] luncheon. Unfortunately, he didn't read the text and only learned the news on a phone call when he was driving home. His passenger quickly put on a mask. Sorry Rich! That is the proverbial "Shutting the barn door after the horse has bolted." Fortunately, Larry and the other ROMEO didn't catch COVID-19 from me.

I never have been a good patient in that I have no patience for being sick. When Larry came home from his outing, he found me on the computer, a box of Kleenex and a cup of tea by my side, interviewing someone for my Holocaust Torah story while typing away. "Get off the damn computer, put on a mask, and go lie down," he told me.

Exhausted, congested, and realizing that I couldn't leave the house anyway, I gave up. I spent the next three days sacked out on the couch catching up on *Outlander*. Note: There is no better way to veg out than spending twenty hours with Jamie and Claire as they romped their way through pre-Revolutionary War America.

Later that evening, Larry made dinner for both of us, something he did every night for the next eight nights. And to top it off, he made me an ice cream sundae every night to help soothe my scratchy throat. At least that is the way we justified 350 calories of pure bliss. Larry, meanwhile, was earning enough "Best Husband in the World" points for a lifetime.

By Sunday, I was feeling well enough to resume writing my upcoming story about Torahs rescued from the Holocaust. I even had enough energy to take a short (masked) walk and to water my drooping houseplants. As was the case for so many others who contracted "the plague;" however, it took me another two weeks to get over the fatigue.

Do I have any regrets about going to the Special Olympics state meet? Not one bit. Seeing our athletes competing in their events, coming down off the awards platform, finding their way to their parents, and beaming with pride, brings so much joy it was worth spending the two days in a sure-fired petri dish. And how could I *not* hug my athletes when they finished a great race or threw the softball farther than they ever had or showed me their medal?

As more and more of my friends and family are coming down with COVID-19, there is in some ways an inevitability.

So where do we go from here? Yes, I may get COVID-19 again, but having it once may have helped me build up some immunity. Larry was spared this round but will he contract it in the future? Only time will tell.

June 23, 2022

Chapter Fifty-One

Venerable or Old? Mature or Elderly?

Outside the window of my grandparents 'apartment on Coney Island Avenue, the subway train zipped past. I watched it as it sped away, wishing it was taking me to the bus station and back to our home 300 miles north on the Canadian border.

I was fifteen years old, and my mother Fran, my sister Bobbie, and I were in the middle of our annual summer visit to our maternal grandparents. Grandma Ethel and Grandpa Joe were in their mid-80s, old by my teenage standards. They were Lithuanian Jewish immigrants, and they had both had hard lives. They conversed with each other and my mother, their "Fradel," in Yiddish, their English passable but unmistakably foreign to American ears. Grandma Ethel was short and soft and wore baggy house dresses and support hose rolled down to her orthopedic shoes. Grandpa Joe was just as short, with stooped shoulders and a scratchy beard. He smelled like a combination of pickled herring, old clothes, and dried urine.

I had just gotten off the phone with a girlfriend, who told me she was having a party that Saturday. Would I be home?

We were scheduled to leave on Sunday, but I begged my mother to leave two days early. A typical teenager, I loved my friends more than my family.

At first my mother refused to change her plans. Grandpa Joe had been increasingly more disoriented and forgetful, showing the first signs of dementia. Grandma Ethel, who had a history of heart problems, seemed particularly frail. In the end, my mother acquiesced to my selfish demands, and the three of us left early Friday morning.

We got back to the North Country in plenty of time for the party. But plans had fallen through, and it had been cancelled. "I guess we could have stayed longer," I told my mom. Mom only shrugged her shoulders.

Late one evening three weeks after we returned, Mom got the phone call she had been dreading. Grandma Ethel had prepared a Shabbat dinner, put the covered challah on the table, lit the two candles in their silver holders, and then sat down for a minute to take a short nap. She never woke up.

My mother flew down to New York the next morning, her first plane ride. When she got there, Grandpa was bereft. "The paramedics hadn't tried hard enough to save her, Fradel!" he cried bitterly. All my mother's attempts to explain that any effort to revive her 83-year-old damaged heart would fail did not heal my grandfather's pain.

Right after the funeral, my parents packed up the remnants of my grandparents' life into the trunk of our station wagon: Grandma Ethel's good china, the Sabbath candlesticks, some photos, and Grandpa's personal belongings. Everything else was given to relatives and friends. We then drove back to the North Country.

With my two older siblings in college, my mother moved Grandpa into my brother Jay's room. Consumed with grief, Grandpa Joe was a sad figure. He spent most of the day sitting on our living room couch, weeping. His only two sources of solace were the car rides on which my mother took him several times a week and my playing Yiddish songs for him on our piano.

For the most part, however, I resented my grandfather's presence. He was old, sad, frequently unshaven, and "smelled funny." One of my most regrettable memories: he was walking around the block to my father's store, and I intentionally walked on the other side of the street as I did not want to be associated with him.

Within a year after Grandma Ethel's death, Grandpa Joe's cognitive abilities had further declined. We had to keep the front door locked after he walked out of the house in the middle of a cold winter's night in his pajamas. His continuing physical decline also made it difficult for my mother to continue as caregiver. Grandpa Joe was moved into a nursing home less than a half mile from our home, where his grief and unhappiness only increased. A few months later, he passed away, happy, I am sure, to be reunited with the love of his life.

As I write this story, Larry and I are in California meeting our six-week-old granddaughter, who is named after my beloved mother, and reuniting with Adam, Sarah, and our two-year-old grandson. We soon will fly to Colorado to spend time with Julie, Sam, and our seven-year-old Mountain Girl. All three of our beautiful grandchildren are young—too young to be more interested in friends than in family. They are hopefully years away from being teenagers who are embarrassed by grandparents who will at that point be not that much younger than Grandma Ethel and Grandpa Joe were the last time I visited them.

Larry and I pride ourselves in being "young" septuagenarians. We can still walk around with our infant granddaughter on our shoulders to help her burp, play on the floor with our San Francisco Kid as he pushes his multiple trucks, and hike with our Mountain Girl up trails close to their Rocky Mountain home. But will they ever look at us in the same way I saw my own grandparents that summer?

Recently, I had a conversation with one of our Special Olympic athletes.

"I am THIRTEEN," he said proudly.

"That's wonderful," I said, "I am a *little* older than you. I am 71."

"That is SO sad," he replied. "Don't you wish you were young again?"

"No," I told him. "I love this age. I have children and grandchildren. I have a lifetime of good memories with plans to make many more."

This brief conversation brought home to me the fact that in the eyes of my grandchildren and yes, other children, we are old. At least six years ago, my niece shared with me her and her husband's concerns regarding the future of "taking care of" her recently widowed mother-in-law as well as her own parents, who are a few years older than us. I told her how glad I was that my own children did not need to have this conversation. "Don't kid yourself, Aunt Marilyn," she told me. "All of us first cousins worry about all of you older people." Ouch!

I have already made Larry promise me that no matter where life takes us, he will make sure that the long hairs that grow on my chin are plucked and I never smell like urine. Meanwhile, I hope that our three grandchildren love us despite how we look or smell or talk. And no matter what, I will love them and their parents to the moon and back.

July 7, 2022

158

Chapter Fifty-Two

From Golden Books To Goldbugs

I am nestled in my mother's arms in a living room chair. As I listen to *Cinderella* and *The Brave Little Tailor*, my two favorites from the Little Golden Books collection, her lap feels different. My four-and-a-half-year status as the youngest Cohen is coming to a close. Soon, my mother will be busy with the new baby. Not long after that, I would be reading on my own. At that moment, however, with my two older siblings at school, I am wrapped up in undivided love.

As a lifetime bookworm, it is no surprise that one of my earliest memories involves my mother reading to me. When Larry and I became parents, we wanted to create these same memories.

Adam's first favorite was also from the Little Golden Books collection. *Corky,* written by Patricia Scarry, recounts the story about a little black dog whose contentious relationship with his boy's favorite teddy bear is redeemed when he finds the lost lovely. We read and re-read that little book until it was held together with scotch tape, hope, and a prayer. *Corduroy,* Don Freeman's classic about nocturnal adventures of a shopworn teddy bear's search for his missing button in a locked department store, became his second choice before lights out.

When we discovered *Go Dog Go,* Larry morphed into the master storyteller. As Adam sat transfixed, Larry emoted each line of P. D Eastman's story about a group of highly mobile dogs who operate every conceivable conveyance in pursuit of work, play, and their final mysterious goal, (SPOILER ALERT) a dog party! Larry's rendition of "Do you like my hat?" is etched into my auditory memory. His asides—"That's so silly!" and "Maybe they are going to the tree to pee?"—kept Adam and, later, Julie entertained for hours. Even today, whenever I see a several canines playing together—a very common sight in Colorado—I repeat Eastman's lines to anyone who will listen: "Big dogs and little dogs and white dogs and black dogs...."

When both children graduated from picture books, Larry and I moved onto chapter books. When Julie was in first grade, I introduced to her *Anne of Green Gables.* She so loved L. M. Montgomery's classic story of a Prince Edward Island orphan that she was reading it on her own by the next year. Her original paperback collection now has a place of honor on her daughter's bookshelf.

The chapter books saga continued on six-hour trips from our home in Upstate New York to our Thanksgiving visits to my siblings in Pennsylvania. The miles flew by as we laughed and commiserated over Peter Hatcher's attempts at dealing with his little brother Fudge in Judy Blume's *Tales of a Fourth Grade Nothing.* Beverly Cleary's *Ramona* series soon followed. We supplemented our own voices with books-on-tape, leading to Adam's discovery and a lifetime love of J. R. R. Tolkien.

The first Harry Potter came out in 2003, years after we stopped reading to our children. Three years later, Larry, Adam, and Julie caravanned cross country. Julie had J. K. Rowling's latest on cassettes, and the two siblings listened together, often leaving Larry to drive solo. They finished in time for her to peel off in Colorado and for Larry and Adam to drive—Potterless—to California.

And then came grandchildren, and this Gammy was glad to read our Mountain Girl classics that she had read to her mother and uncle. She soon had her own copies of *Corky, Corduroy,* and *Cinderella.* Her Zayde gladly read her *Go Dog Go,* complete with asides and exaggerated, emotive expositions.

By 2015, a new group of classics had appeared on the scene. I, even more than our Mountain Girl, fell in love with William Stieg's *Sylvester and the Magic Pebble.* I teared up every time the little donkey, who had accidentally turned himself into a rock, reappears as himself and knows that no desire is more important than a family's love. Since my college Kiddie Lit course, I had loved the illustrations of Paul Zelinsky and purchased several of his books so I could share the artwork with my granddaughter. After reading Anna Dewdney's *Llama Llama Red Pajama,* I stopped some of her potential tantrums by laughingly requesting that she stop her "llama drama."

During the pandemic, we were unable to see our Mountain Girl in person for over 14 months. Thank goodness for FaceTime! Ever since she was three years old, Larry had spent hours telling his granddaughter his creative stories about an entire cast of denizens of the forest, including the Big Bad Wolf, his wife Wendy, and their triplets; the mayor of the forest Morty Moose and his wife Marion; and an imported Florida alligator named Allie. The Mountain Girl connected with us on social media for up to four to five hours a week to hear his increasingly outlandish tales. When Larry's voice gave out, I took over with either library or purchased books, culminating in my reading and then re-reading to her the entire Ramona/Beezus collection.

Our San Francisco Kid was born the week the pandemic closed down his city. By the time he was two, he was fully engaged in playing with, watching, wearing, and reading anything about trucks. *Go Dog Go* was an early favorite as Eastman's dogs were illustrated in every mode of transportation. Then he discovered Richard Scarry's *Cars, Trucks, and Things That Go.* During our recent visit, we watched as he poured over the pictures with the fervor of a *Yeshiva* student pouring over his *Talmudic* tractates. When I learned that a tiny goldbug was hidden on each page, I became obsessed with finding them. I then passed that obsession onto my grandson. "Goldbug!" he would shout when we located one, and we would slap each other five. A week after we left, Adam reported that his son had mastered finding the goldbug on every page, each discovery accompanied by "Goldbug!" and a high five.

As our second granddaughter was born seven weeks prematurely this past spring, she is obviously a long way from understanding the power of reading. As she was named after my mother, I will be supplying her with all the books in Russell Hoban's *Frances the Badger* series. The stories have no trucks, but hopefully her big brother will like them anyway. And I will make sure she always has a copy of *Fradel's Story,* the book I co-wrote with my mother and her namesake.

This past week, our Mountain Girl celebrated her seventh birthday. As Uncle Adam and Aunt Sarah watched on FaceTime, she unwrapped their presents—Adam's favorite, *The Lord of the Rings* and, on Julie's suggestion, *His Dark Materials* trilogy with its strong female protagonist.

  After everyone signed off, our Colorado family cracked open Tolkien, our San Francisco family searched for Scarry's Goldbug, and Gammy and Zayde *kvelled* that the joys of reading to children aloud—whether it be Golden books or *Go Dog Go* or goldbugs.

July 21, 2022

Chapter Fifty-Three

Meshugganah Summer

This was, to say the least, a different summer in the Rockies. No matter how well one can plan for time away, life still happens. *Meshugganah*!

After eight wonderful days in California with Adam's family, we flew into Denver and then headed for Julie's home in Summit County. While unpacking, I realized my Kindle was lost in transit. I wish I had been able to brush the loss off as a human error, but I spent too much time trying to track it down (no luck at Southwest Airlines, either airport, or Enterprise), deciding on whether to order a replacement (thank goodness for a well-timed Amazon Prime Day sale) and beating myself up for losing it in the first place.

Although Summit County normally experiences the monsoon season in late July, this year it started soon after we arrived. Two days were complete washouts, but weather came in most days in early afternoon. As a result, most evening outdoor concerts, a favorite summer activity we have done in the past with family and friends, were cancelled.

Meanwhile, as has happened throughout the country, this very contagious coronavirus variant hit Summit County hard—and close to home. On July 1, the day we moved into our rental, we stocked up on groceries at City Market, along with many other maskless vacationers. We brought home chicken, produce, ingredients for challah baking, and COVID-19. By July 3, Larry was feeling under the weather; by July 5, he tested positive.

My May encounter with the nasty virus gave me some immunity from this variant, but Larry was not spared. He was down for the count for five days and, as he was still testing positive, isolated for five more. He missed out on our Mountain Girl's birthday party, several trips to Main Street to get her mango bubble tea, and many games of Sorry! FaceTime may be a blessing when we are in Florida; it was a poor substitute when our rental was literally a stone's throw from their house.

We also both passed on the planned weekend getaway with Sam's family in Granby, Colorado. Sam's parents, Marilyn and Bill, who are also our dear friends, cancelled their second attempt to see us when Larry was hit by a mean head cold.

Although I had hiked almost every day during Larry's illness by just walking out of our rental, we were able to take our first hike together two and half weeks into our stay. Outside of my taking another one of my famous pratfalls on one; Larry being attacked by mosquitos despite the bug spray on the second; our almost getting caught in a thunderstorm on the third; and encountering a snake on the fourth, we finally were able to spend quality time together on the trail.

By this time, Larry was well past COVID-19 and colds. On July 21, Marilyn and Bill drove up from Fort Collins with plans for the seven of us to attend the National Repertory Orchestra's annual pop concert in nearby Breckinridge. An hour before we were supposed to leave, the Mountain Girl came home from the fourth day of science camp with a live jellyfish and a lively case of COVID-19. The four grandparents went to the concert while Julie and Sam stayed home. Wisely, Marilyn and Bill drove the two hours back home immediately following the concert to avoid further exposure. The parents, however, were not so lucky. All three—five if you include the dog and "Jelly"—were now in quarantine. Sigh! We were back to FaceTime visits.

Meanwhile, a funny thing happened on our way to the Lake Dillon Theater. Soon after the NRO family no-go, we got an email stating both musicals for which we had purchased tickets were cancelled due to a COVID-19 outbreak among the cast and staff. Yes, any live indoor performances in any "forum" were just an "impossible dream."

And yet, despite lost electronics; despite monsoons, despite curtailed concerts and cancelled curtain calls; despite pratfalls and pests and the pandemic, Larry and I remained focused on the positive (no pun intended). We squeezed in many healthy, happy moments with our granddaughter.

Several mornings, with the help of FaceTime, Larry and I followed the Tour de France with Adam (who loves cycling) and our grandson (who kept asking for Elmo on the "TV"). For eight nights, Larry and I watched historical wins at the World Track and Field Championships out of Eugene Oregon (Go Sydney McLaughlin! Go Armand Duplantis!). I researched future stories, wrote articles, worked on this book, and updated my blog. Once healthy, Larry resumed playing pickleball with the Summit County pickleball club ("We play with an altitude!"), along with taking several more hikes with me. Thanks to the local library and my new Kindle, I read lots of books. And even though Southwest Airlines has yet to locate my old Kindle, I was assured by a lovely woman in the Denver office that as it is one of 9000 items accumulated by the central lost and found office, I have a good chance of it being recovered by Hanukkah (*Chag Sameach*, Larry! You have been regifted!)

By the time we left the mountains, all my family members had completely recovered from COVID-19. We were safe and in one piece. We did not have to cancel entire vacations due to illnesses, a fate that befell two close relatives. We are not grieving and traumatized like so many families in Buffalo, Ulvalde, Highland Park, and other sites of senseless violence. And no matter what the weather, we spent six weeks basking in the beauty and cooler temperatures of the Colorado Rockies.

Furthermore, as I have done since the beginning of the pandemic, I kept calm and baked challah. On a Sunday afternoon, as a torrential rainstorm raged outside our balcony, I cooked up dinner for my quarantined family— chicken, rice, carrots, and two freshly baked braided loaves. I kneaded in prayers for their quick recovery and prayers of gratitude for all the joy and happiness and love we have experienced this very different summer.

August 4, 2022

Chapter Fifty-Four

Thunderstorms

When I was six years old, I loved summer storms. As the sky turned dark, the thunder clapped, and the lightning shot across the sky, I would watch from the safety of our living room window. My mother assured me that the noise was just God bowling.

When I was sixteen, I loved summer storms. By that time, my parents had purchased a cottage on Willsboro Bay in Upstate New York. From the safety of our porch, I would watch the rain come down in sheets and the waves rock our boat that was moored 200 yards offshore.

When we moved to Florida, I still loved summer storms. But I soon learned to respect their intensity and duration. Our state has as many as 100 stormy days a year, and our climate means that these storms can happen any month of the year. Florida also has the dubious honor of being the lightning capital of the United States. I have been witness to their fury again and again from the safety of our lanai. And on several occasions, I have had to take shelter quickly as the weather changed too quickly for me to realize what was coming.

Over seven years after our move, I now see these storms as a reminder of how fragile our lives can be.

On a beautiful morning in July 2017, a group of fellow residents were playing golf on the course in our 55+ community. Suddenly, the sky darkened as huge black clouds moved in. The golfers, all seasoned Florida residents, knew what to do. They abandoned their game and headed for their golf carts and shelter.

It was too late. A bolt of lightning struck two of the men. One was thrown to the ground, shaken but okay. The second person was struck full force, and the electricity travelled through his body. By the time he was brought to the hospital, he was brain dead. The doctors kept him on life support long enough for his devastated wife and children to say their goodbyes.

What are the chances of getting hit by lightning? According to Wikipedia, it is one in 700,000. For my neighbor, the odds were 1:1.

What happened to the couple that fateful morning? Did they give each other a kiss before he headed out the door? And what were their last words to one another? "I love you! See you later." Or was their conversation ordinary and mundane? "We need to pick up some milk," or "The Red Sox are playing the Yankees tonight." Or were their last words that she regretted? "You promised you would fix that leaky faucet!"

Larry and I are both in our seventies. The specter of death hangs over us a little more heavily than it did twenty—or even ten—years ago. People we know die suddenly from heart attacks or slowly from cancer. Since February 2020, the emergence and staying power of COVID-19 resulted in a million deaths in the United States alone, with too many friends part of the devastating numbers. As I write this essay, Florida is reeling from the impact of Hurricane Ian, whose swath of destruction and horrific flooding is being called an unprecedented catastrophe. The number of deaths is unknown. It is already recognized that many fatalities would have been avoided if every individual had either heeded recommended evacuation orders and/or sheltered inside until it was safe to venture out. No matter, each death is a sad reminder of how our lives can change on a dime.

Sad, but not tragic. To me, tragic is the death of a 31-year-old daughter to leukemia. Tragic is losing a nineteen-year-old granddaughter to a car accident on a rainy night one block from her home. Tragic is losing a sixteen-year-old grandson who had been severely disabled since he was a baby. And tragic is losing a husband from—literally— a bolt out of the blue.

Biz hundert un tzvantsig!—May you live to 120!—is a popular Jewish blessing for a long healthy life. Each loss, whether the number of years were short or long, whether a death was sad or tragic, is my personal reminder to treat each moment with gratitude. "Life is so transient and ephemeral; we will not be here after a breath," said Dr. Debasish Mridha, an American physician and philosopher. "So, think better, think deeply, think with kindness, and write it with love so that it may live a little longer."

Some of us are fortunate enough to live a great deal longer. My mother's first cousin Eli Helfand passed away in 2018, three months after his 100th birthday. A World War II veteran and a graduate of Clarkson College, Eli spent almost all his working life in Richfield Springs, New York, where he owned and operated Ruby's Department Store. He had two wonderful marriages, raised four strong, independent children, and got to enjoy his five grandchildren and two great-grandchildren.

What I remember most about my cousin Eli are our strong family connections. During the Depression, when his parents were struggling to get their Upstate New York store afloat, Eli spent summers and school vacations with my mother and her family in New York City. He introduced my parents to each other and served as best man at their wedding. Eli drove the car that the newlyweds took from the city to Alburgh, Vermont. Mom shared the front seat with Eli's mother Rose while my father sat in the back seat with all the wedding presents, including a floor lamp that Bill had to hold for the eight-hour trip. My parents remained close to Eli and Florence, who attended my parents '60th anniversary. When Florence passed away and Eli

remarried, he and his second wife Marty became an integral part of not only my parents 'life but also of mine. We visited them at their homes in Otsego County in New York as well as their retirement home in Englewood, Florida.

Eli and I shared another close connection. His daughter Marsha and I are only weeks apart in age. We spent time with each other as children as well as our four years as students at University at Albany. We have attended each other's weddings as well as those of our children.

In August 1962, I spent a week with Marsha and her family at their cottage on Canadarago Lake. We played and replayed Ray Stevens 'what now would be considered politically incorrect song about "Ahab the Arab, the sheik of the golden sand." We baked cookies. We went swimming and boating. And when the storm clouds moved in, we ran back inside. From the porch windows, we watched the lightning flash across the sky and listened to the thunder echo off the surrounding hills. We turned the Ray Stevens record back on and danced around the living room in our bare feet. We were safe in the childhood belief that life would treat us kind and that we would live forever—or at least *"hundert un tzvantsig"* years.

Originally published February 1, 2020.
Updated for this book.

167

Chapter Fifty-Five

Keep Calm And Bake Challah Redux

I t is 7 a.m. on a sunny September morning in Florida. For the first time in several weeks, we are not on the road. I am ready to resume my pandemic ritual of baking challah. We are having a friend over for a Shabbat dinner. And, more importantly, two people I know are going through chemotherapy. I am motivated to bring the fresh warm loaves to them before sunset.

It is now two and a half years almost to the day since the world closed down because of COVID-19. Soon after, I decided that having a Sabbath meal every Friday would bring Larry and me joy. I polished Grandma Annie's candlesticks; bought a new Kiddish cup on eBay (I must have lost mine in our move); brought out my embroidered challah cover and located Flo Miller's recipe I had always meant to try. With some difficulty—the whole world had decided along with me to make bread—I purchased flour, yeast, and sugar to make the traditional Shabbat bread. Then I mixed and kneaded and braided four small loaves. I shared one with the president of our shuttered synagogue and one with a friend whose wife had just been placed in memory care.

By April, I had totally embraced not only the baking elements but also the spiritual elements. I learned that it was appropriate to say a *Mi Shebeirach,* a prayer of physical and emotional healing, during the kneading process. I frequently played Debbie Friedman's beautiful musical rendition as I kneaded the pliant, soft dough. I opened my iPhone to the ever-changing, never-ending list of people who needed prayers. My cousin with pancreatic cancer A friend who lost his wife to lung cancer. Another friend who lost her daughter to suicide. And, on a more hopeful note, a young couple who were trying to buy their first home. (They moved in this summer!)

We developed a rhythm: Every Friday afternoon I baked the challahs. Just before sunset, Larry would head off in our car, delivering two or three still warm fragrant loaves to needy people in our community. When I couldn't physically share them, I took pictures and attached them to an email with a note. "So sorry you are going through this. I kneaded prayers of healing into this loaf of bread. Thinking of you. Love, Marilyn."

By the time Larry and I were finally able to travel to see our children and grandchildren in June 2021, I was a seasoned challah maker—to a point. Baking bread in someone else's kitchen proved to be a challenge. I scurried to find the measuring cups and spoons and the right sized bowls. In San Francisco, the sound of the Mixmaster creaming the butter in the initial steps of the challah process woke my grandson from his nap. In Colorado, the 9100-foot elevation resulted in loaves that looked more like amoebas. No matter what the elevation, Larry said my crusts were too soft.

Therefore, I tweaked my technique. I replaced the butter with canola oil, which meant less noise and more kneading time, my favorite part of the experience. Rocky Mountain challahs needed to go into the oven immediately after braiding to prevent over-rising. A straight egg yolk wash resulted in browner, shinier loaves, of which Larry wholeheartedly approved. "This is the way challah is *supposed* to crunch," he said, biting into a warm crunchy slice.

Friends have asked me if they could buy my challahs or if I would consider selling them at our community's Farmer's Market. I declined, telling them emphatically I am not starting a new career. Instead, I offer them my challah recipe, complete with additional tips.

This past spring, I invited two friends over for a challah-making workshop. After we all enjoyed slices of the warm loaves smothered with butter, Ann and Trudi went home with a batch of the still-rising dough they had prepared. Later that evening, they sent me pictures of their beautiful, finished creations. I am just following an old Yiddish expression: "Give people a challah, and they eat for a day. Give them a recipe, and they become challah bakers!" (Okay. I made that up.)

As our world has opened up, finding the time to make the challahs on Friday has been more difficult. I sometimes cheat by planning ahead and by making seven or eight loaves. I freeze a few braided unbaked challahs to be defrosted and baked when needed. I still feel Jewish guilt when I use that shortcut.

***

On March 25, 2020, I published my first "pandemic" story in Capital Region of New York's *The Jewish World*. "As I write this, we are in the second week of our own national crisis," I stated. "Larry and I worry about our friends and family—especially our own children." Over the ensuing months, I wrote about how COVID-19 and its forced locked-down impacted us: our first sad Passover seder for two; our hours and hours on Zoom; our trimmed down wardrobe (on my not slimming down body); our hopes for a more sensible approach to COVID-19 with a new president; our tentative steps back into the world with masks and bottles of hand sanitizer and vaccines and boosters; our joy in finally reuniting with our children and grandchildren; our own encounters with the illness (along with alligators and moose and jellyfish); and, of course, my kneading and shaping the dozens of loaves of challahs I baked throughout the long months. Looking back, I can gratefully say that we have survived the pandemic, politics, pratfalls, and other of life's *tsouris*—problems. Hope is now within reach. A September 19, 2022, Reuters article reported that the director of the World Health Organization declared the end of the pandemic is in sight. It was the most optimistic assessment from the UN agency since it declared an international emergency in January 2020.

Larry and I are feeling that optimism. Yes, we will mask when necessary, especially in unavoidable crowded venues. Yes, we will test if exposed, showing symptoms, or asked. Yes, we will keep up with our boosters. But we are moving on. We are going to plays, eating inside at restaurants, attending weddings in Massachusetts and Mexico. We are learning to navigate the new normal in the Age of COVID-19.

No matter how I do it, I will continue to keep calm and bake challah.

L'Chaim!
October 1, 2022

Marilyn's Challah Recipe

Ingredients

5 1/2 - 6 cups King Arthur all-purpose flour (divided)
1/2 cup canola oil
1 1/2 cups boiling water
4 1/2 teaspoons LeSaffre Saf-Instant Yeast, Gold
1/2 cup Domino sugar
1/2 teaspoon salt
3 eggs (2 for batter; one yolk for egg wash)
Extra canola oil for greasing bowls
Optional: ½ to ¾ cup raisins

Directions

1. In a large bowl, combine two cups flour, yeast, sugar, and salt.
2. Add water/oil mixture, which should be very warm. Mix with spatula until it is a smooth batter.
3. Add one cup flour. Mix until smooth.
4. Add two eggs. Mix until smooth.
5. Gradually add two more cups flour, mixing with your hands or a spatula. Incorporate enough flour so you can form a ball.
6. Turn the ball onto a lightly floured surface. (I use my kitchen counter for this.)
7. Knead the dough for approximately ten minutes, adding flour as needed. This is when I think good thoughts about my family and say prayers for those who need it.
8. Optional: Knead in raisins if desired.
9. Lightly grease a large bowl with two to three teaspoons of canola oil. Put dough into bowl, turning greased side up. Cover with a light tea towel and put in a warm spot. Allow the dough to rise for 1 ½ to 2 hours or until double in bulk.
10. Preheat the oven to 350°F.
11. Punch down the dough. Turn it onto a lightly floured surface. Knead the dough a few times, throwing it hard onto the counter a couple of times to get out air bubbles and to work off any of the week's tension.

12. Divide the dough into sections. I usually divide the dough into three loaves, but you can choose to make two big ones or four small ones. Braid each bread. I usually start with three ropes for each bread. Talented people can do more!
13. Grease cookie sheets and line with silicone mats or parchment paper. Place loaves on mats.
14. In a small cup, beat the remaining egg with one tablespoon of water. Brush each loaf with the egg wash.
15. Let rise for an additional 15-30 minutes as needed. Don't let it over-rise!
16. Bake at 350°F for 30 minutes. Time will vary according to size. Bread is done when it has reached an internal temperature of 210°F. It will be brown on both top and underside.
17. Remove from oven and place on racks to cool. *Shabbat Shalom!*

Thanks to Flo Miller from Clifton Park, New York; Carol Nathan from San Francisco, California; and Jamie Geller, the "Jewish Rachel Ray," from Israel for their recipes that are reflected in amounts and/or processes. I also recommend **Rising: The Book of Challah** by Rochie Pinson (Feldheim Publishers, 2017) for more recipes, braiding techniques, and inspiration.

Photographs and Illustrations

"Keep Calm and Bake Challah" apron was created by Keep Calm Maker: Designs and Collections on Zazzle

Chapter 2: Yiddish: Courtesy of BigStock.com.

Chapter 3: Passover: Courtesy of Rebecca Silverstein.

Chapter 5: Hemingway Courtesy Wikimedia Commons. Ernest-Hemingway-with-cat-1954.jpg

Chapter 8: What I Miss Most. Courtesy Wikimedia Commons. https://commons.wikimedia.org/wiki/File:Question_mark_1.svg

Chapter 9: Silver Linings: Courtesy of BigStock.com

Chapter 10: George Floyd: Courtesy Wikimedia Commons Wandbild Portrait George Floyd von Eme Street Art im Mauerpark (Berlin).jpg

Chapter 13: Courtesy of *The Jewish World*

Chapter 15: Be Ruth-Less: Courtesy Wikimedia Commons. Ruth_Bader_Ginsburg,_official_SCOTUS_portrait,_crop.jpg

Chapter 16: Measure for Measure: Courtesy Wikimedia Commons. TRUMP_DEATH_CLOCK_2_051920.jpg

Chapter 18: I Can Breathe: Courtesy Wikimedia Commons. Joe_Biden_official_portrait_2013_cropped_(cropped)

Chapter 19: Hallmark Christmas: Courtesy of BigStock.com

Chapter 21: Wintering Through the Pandemic. Courtesy Wikimedia Commons. Ian Bradbury. Winter scene - geograph.org.uk - 3563710.jpg

Chapter 23: WWE: Courtesy of Wikimedia Commons. WWE_black_logo.svg.png

Chapter 24: Scarlett Letter. Courtesy Wikimedia Commons. Hester_Prynne.jpeg

Chapter 28: Bok Tower: https://commons.wikimedia.org/wiki/User:Sandhill_Gopher author

Chapter 29: Wasabi Courtesy Wikimedia Commons. 640px-Sushi_(26571132695).jpg

Chapter 30: Fish Friday. Courtesy Wikimedia Commons. 640px-fried_smelt_food_ dinner_\cooked.jpg

Chapter 38: Mountain Mama. Courtesy Ash Weisel.

Chapter 43: Planting Trees. Courtesy Wikimedia Commons. Tree_planting_in_Ghana_9.jpg

Chapter 45: Lifetime Achievement Awards. Image courtesy of https://clipground.com

Chapter 47: Pickleball Putz: Free-Pickleball-clipart-1.pn

Chapter 49: Happy Wherever I Am. Golden Gate Bridge by David Mark from pixabay.com

Larry and Marilyn Shapiro

About the Author

MARILYN COHEN SHAPIRO grew up in a very close-knit family in a small town on Lake Champlain. Since retiring from a career in adult education in Upstate New York and relocating to Florida, she is now writing down her family's stories as well as the accounts of ordinary people with extraordinary lives. She and her husband Larry are proud to have raised two children who enjoy reading, learning, and traveling as much as they do. Marilyn loves singing along to Broadway musicals, getting lost on well-marked trails in national parks, and eating vanilla ice cream.

Marilyn has been a regular contributor to the bi-weekly publication, *The Jewish World* (Capital Region, New York), since 2013. Her articles have also been published in the *Heritage Florida Jewish News* and several websites including the *Union of Reform Judaism, Jewish War Veterans of the United States of America, Growing Bolder, and Jewish Women of Words (Australia).* She is the author of three previous compilations of stories, **There Goes My Heart** (2016); **Tikkun Olam: Stories of Repairing an Unkind World.** (2018) and **Fradel's Story** (cowritten with her mother Frances Cohen, 2021).

She is working on her fifth book, *Under the Shelter of Butterfly Wings: Stories of Jewish Sacrifice, Survival, and Strength,* a collection of memoirs of Jewish Holocaust survivors, soldiers, and other individuals with extraordinary stories to share.

Her books are available on Amazon in both paperback and Kindle format.

Her blog is: http://theregoesmyheart.me/

You may email her at: shapcomp18@gmail.com

Made in the USA
Columbia, SC
26 October 2024

44723092R00098